100 Masterpieces of Design
from the collections of the Centre Pompidou

Centre
Pompidou

© Éditions du Centre
Pompidou, Paris, 2011

ISBN: 978-2-84426-475-6
Publisher number: 1440
Copyright registration:
september 2011

Front cover (left to right):
Pierre Chareau,
Floor Lamp, known as the
"Grande Religieuse," 1923
Eileen Gray,
Bathroom Cupboard, 1927-1929
Charles Eames, Ray Eames,
Paw Chair, 1948
Marc Newson,
Alufelt Chair, 1993

100
Masterpieces
of Design

Edited by
Françoise Guichon and Frédéric Migayrou

With texts by
Marielle Dagault
Xavier de Jarcy
Marie-Thérèse Mazel-Roca
Cloé Pitiot
Odile Rousseau
Pierre Tillet
Anne-Marie Zucchelli

Preface

If design is attracting increasing interest not only among collectors
and aficionados, but also in terms of the creation of new institutional
projects – museums, resource centres and exhibitions – this is, of course,
in response to the demands of a growing public. The proliferation
of specialist fairs and auctions, the expansion of educational
opportunities and the emergence of new careers: all testify to
the emergence of a distinctive field of culture. Though it included from
the beginning a Centre for Industrial Design (the Centre de Création
Industrielle) alongside the National Museum of Modern Art (the Musée
National d'Art Moderne), the Centre Pompidou did not establish a specific
collection until 1992, when Dominique Bozo, then president of the Centre,
initiated two specialist collections, within the Museum, devoted
to architecture and design. In twenty years, the design collection has won
for itself a place in the first rank on the international stage through
the wealth of its holdings – evident in the successive presentations
of the Museum's permanent collections. Its importance is confirmed
by the continuous demand for loans to major exhibitions elsewhere.
An active acquisitions policy, aimed at the creation of coherent ensembles,
as well as gifts from designers and from the Société des Amis du Musée,
together with donations in lieu of tax – one such bringing us the major
works of Pierre Chareau – continue to strengthen a vast collection that
is as attentive to French design as it is open to the international scene.
The selection of a hundred masterpieces from a field as wide and
as various can only be an arbitrary exercise. In addition to featuring
the pieces that already enjoy a world-wide reputation, it has been
a matter of highlighting works, often unique, that represent milestones
in the history of design, among them the prototype *Grand Confort Chair*
by Le Corbusier, Perriand and Jeanneret, Eileen Gray's *Bathroom Cupboard*
(1927-1929), Pierre Chareau's *Desk for Robert Mallet-Stevens* (1927),
Carlo Mollino's *Desk* (1950), Verner Panton's *Living Sculpture* (1970-1971),
Ettore Sottsass's *Altare (Molto Privato)* (1968), and Luigi Colani's *Racing
Motorcycle* (1986). It has also been to draw attention to historic pieces not
well enough known, such as Francis Jourdain's *Rail-Mounted Furniture*
(1927-1928) and Pierre Paulin's *Déclive* (1968), and to experimental creations
of the recent past, such as Ron Arad's *Oh-Void* (2006) and Joris Laarman's
Lounge Chair (2006). Elaborating connections between past and present,
all these choices represent possible means of approach, introductions
to a dynamic collection; a collection that is in continuous development,
so that any future list of a hundred masterpieces, we may be sure, could
be very different.

Alfred Pacquement
*Director of the Musée National d'Art Moderne-Centre
de Création Industrielle*

Recollections

Established in 1992, the Centre Pompidou's design collection focused at first on a nucleus of iconic works, essential landmarks in the 20th-century history of the discipline. It has since then developed considerably, solidly anchored around the holdings of particular designers and movements that give it its distinctive profile as compared to other major collections across the world. With almost 8,000 works, it today covers all the periods and stylistic movements of the 20th century, including the most recent fields of research and experiment in design. Central to the mission of the Musée National d'Art Moderne, design finds itself here in direct dialogue with one of the largest and most extensive collections of modern and contemporary art in the world, not to mention the sizeable architecture collection, it too established in 1992. Many architects, like Le Corbusier, Marcel Breuer, Alvar Aalto, Arne Jacobsen, Jean Prouvé and Carlo Mollino, were in fact major figures in the field of industrial design, responsible for the promotion of the innovative, functionalist aesthetic that accompanied the very establishment of design as an autonomous discipline. Yet if the aesthetic movements that have animated design had their echoes in other artistic domains, the very idea of a design collection long appeared problematic, seemingly contradicted by the nature of the objects: part work of art, part functional artefact.

When Nikolaus Pevsner published his *Pioneers of the Modern Movement* in 1936, he sought to bring out the new role of the designer in the industrial process. His Birmingham study, *An Enquiry into Industrial Art in England*, followed upon a careful analysis of the German Werkbund. It laid down the premises of an industrial archaeology that conferred foundational status not only on the architecture of Walter Gropius but on Peter Behrens's designs for AEG. Beyond a reading in terms of the successive aesthetic movements of modernity (Arts & Crafts, Werkbund, Bauhaus), Pevsner accorded to industrial artefacts an aesthetic status – a value within a distinctive field of creative endeavour – that itself made them available to a historical understanding in which they were no longer simply "antiquities" but agents, direct testimony to an effort of creative conception. The pre-eminence that Pevsner grants to Gropius, director of the Bauhaus and proponent of an industrial modernity based on the active cooperation of the disciplines, and more especially of a seamless continuity between fine and applied arts, reflects a reading of history in which design comes into its creative rights. The bentwood process of furniture manufacture used by Thonet and the appearance of bent metal tube in the work of Mart Stam and Marcel Breuer become milestones in the institution of a modernity understood as a radical break with the past, characterised by functionalism and an abstraction based on the use of new materials.

The first museum design collection, begun by Alfred H. Barr, director of New York's Museum of Modern Art in 1932, and the "Machine Art" exhibition staged there in 1934, confirmed this extension of the field of art history, now open to industrial production. But it was another idea of history that presided over the establishment of the Centre de Création Industrielle (CCI) in 1969. The new institution was intended as an observatory of industrial production informed by a sociology of usage, as witnessed by the exhibitions from 1971 to 1975, devoted to "Tools," "The Meal," "Material, Technology, Form," and "Mechanised Places." The integration of the CCI into the project of the Centre Georges Pompidou involved two major orientations: its opening to sociological and critical thinking, with, for example, the foundation of the journal *Traverses*, and the development of a kind of design promotion agency, based on a research and information unit devoted to product design, which organised more than 200 exhibitions between 1977 and 1992, half of them focussing on design practice. From 1984, on the initiative of François Burkhardt, himself the author of a standard work on the Werkbund, there was a shift towards historical and monographic exhibitions, ever more clearly emphasizing the distinctive creative identities of past and present practitioners, whether architects or designers.

With this background, nourished by the historical and critical approaches adopted from the first by the Centre de Création Industrielle, the design collection of the Musée National d'Art Moderne has developed around a more archaeological than historical understanding that focuses, beyond the object itself, on the project it represents. Like architecture, design answers to a programme, and only attention to the mass of drawings, prototypes, variants and materials allows the reconstruction of the logic of conception and design that has then to be contextualised, situated aesthetically and sociologically. The gradual expansion of the design collection has thus aimed at the constitution of ensembles of objects that help render legible the complexity and distinctiveness of the work of a designer or movement. Around a nucleus of essential pieces by Alvar Aalto, Marcel Breuer, Le Corbusier, Mies van der Rohe, Gerrit Rietveld, Charles Eames, George Nelson, Harry Bertoia and others, groups of works and documents have been assembled that offer various types of readings of the collection. While a great number of industrial products have been acquired, certain areas of the collection have been more specifically developed along regional lines: Italian design (Giuseppe Pagano, Gio Ponti, Osvaldo Borsani, Achille and Pier Giacomo Castiglioni, Carlo Mollino, Joe Colombo, Gaetano Pesce, Gino Sarfatti, Marco Zanuso and others); Scandinavian design (Alvar Aalto, Arne Jacobsen, Poul Kjærholm, Hans Wegner...); and of course French design (Pierre Paulin, Pierre Guariche, Olivier Mourgue, Roger Tallon...).

Today, the collection is internationally renowned for the number of pieces, often unique, that it holds for each creator. For such figures as Eileen Gray, Pierre Chareau, Jean Prouvé, Ettore Sottsass, Serge Mouille, Michele De Lucchi and Philippe Starck, the Centre Pompidou has come to play an irreplaceable role, both in lending to countless exhibitions and as a resource for researchers. Other exceptional holdings, documenting movements, ensure great historical scope to the collection. Among these, for instance, are the hundred or so pieces associated with the movement central to the institution of French Modernism, the Union des Artistes Modernes (UAM), whose leading members, such as Charlotte Perriand, Pierre Chareau, Eileen Gray, Robert Mallet-Stevens and Jean Prouvé, have now become world-famous, somewhat overshadowing such figures as Francis Jourdain, René Herbst and Djo-Bourgeois. Like the sets of Marcel Breuer chairs and of L.C. series furniture by Le Corbusier, Perriand and Jeanneret, the acquisition of the most copied bar stool ever and its attribution to Louis Sognot underlines the important work of historical linkage that the collection makes possible. Another significant European holding represents the Italian Radical Architecture movement, whose emphasis on the environment – the *ambiente* – and on a new relation between body and space is still an influence on today's design. Alongside a substantial holding of Sottsass that includes key pieces from every period of his career, there are major ensembles by Superstudio, Ugo La Pietra, Haus-Rucker-Co, Michele De Lucchi and others. Concerned both with recent history and with the remembrance of objects, usages and technologies of production, the design collection, more than any other, represents a form of provisional memory, weaving connections between the works of the present and those of the past.

Frédéric Migayrou
Deputy Director of the Musée National d'Art Moderne,
Responsible for Industrial Design

Otto Wagner . Peter Behrens . Atelier Gras . Pierre Chareau . Joost Schmidt
Josef Hartwig . Marcel Breuer . Jacques Le Chevallier . Robert Mallet-
Stevens . Henri Liber . Charlotte Perriand . Francis Jourdain . Eileen Gray
Le Corbusier . Pierre Jeanneret . Giuseppe Pagano . Djo-Bourgeois . René
Herbst . Louis Sognot . Jean Prouvé . Émile Guillot . André Lurçat . Alvar
Aalto . Gerrit Rietveld . Eugène Beaudouin . Marcel Lods . Gio Ponti . René
Coulon . Hans Coray . Bruno Mathsson . Eero Saarinen . Charles Eames
Ray Eames . Bic . Carlo Mollino . Hans J . Wegner . Marco Zanuso . Harry
Bertoia . Janette Laverrière . Poul Kjærholm . Serge Mouille . Willy Guhl
Gino Sarfatti . Isamu Noguchi . Osvaldo Borsani . Poul Henningsen . Janine
Abraham . Dirk Jan Rol . George Nelson . Arne Jacobsen . Pierre Guariche
Achille Castiglioni . Pier Giacomo Castiglioni . Dieter Rams . Joe Colombo
Roger Tallon . Olivier Mourgue . Richard Sapper . Pierre Paulin . Gae
Aulenti . Haus-Rucker-Co . Marc Held . Ugo La Pietra . Archizoom Associati
Ettore Sottsass . Superstudio . Mario Bellini . Shiro Kuramata . Verner
Panton . Jean Widmer . Oscar Niemeyer . Gaetano Pesce . Michel Cadestin
Alessandro Mendini . Roman Cieslewicz . Garouste & Bonetti . Martin
Szekely . Michele De Lucchi . Philippe Starck . Luigi Colani . Andrea Branzi
Marc Newson . Maarten Van Severen . James Dyson . Ronan & Erwan
Bouroullec . Tokujin Yoshioka . Patrick Jouin . Junya Ishigami
Demakersvan . Ron Arad . Louise Campbell . Pierre Charpin . Joris Laarman

Otto Wagner

1841, Penzing (Austria)
1918, Vienna (Austria)

• • • • • • • • • • • • • • • •

In the early years of the 20th century, Austrian architect Otto Wagner designed the furniture for the buildings he put up in Vienna. His teaching at the city's Academy of Fine Arts had provided the theoretical and practical principles informing the Viennese architecture and furniture design of the day, contributing to the establishment of the Secession in 1897.

This bentwood chair developed between 1900 and 1906 is closely related to those that Wagner designed for the newsroom of the daily *Die Zeit* (manufactured by J. & J. Kohn in 1902) and for the offices and public spaces of the Vienna Postsparkasse, built and

fitted out between 1904 and 1906 (manufactured by Thonet). Like them, it has a frame of steam-bent wood that forms the armrests and the four legs, joined by a hoop stretcher beneath the seat. The seat and backrest are formed of sheets of plywood, that of the backrest being perforated. Wagner made use of industrial materials and techniques, and all superfluous ornament has disappeared, the surface being enlivened by the graphic vigour of the holes alone, while the play of the curved lines emphasizes the constructional principles of a form born of function.

The chair was produced by the Austrian company J. & J. Kohn, a specialist since 1868 in the production of bentwood furniture, for domestic use particularly. In 1924, Kohn merged with Mundus AG, and the new company itself merged with Thonet in 1922 • **AMZ**

➜ **1900-1906**

Chair
Manufacturer: J. & J. Kohn (Austria)
Bent wood and plywood
83 x 47 x 58 cm
Accession, 1993
AM 1993-1-857

• •

⬆ **1909-1910**

Electric Kettle
Manufacturer: AEG (Germany)
Nickel-plated brass and rattan
20 cm (h) x 15 cm (ø), 1 l (capacity)
Gift of the Société des Amis du Musée National d'Art Moderne (Paris, France), 2000
AM 2000-1-3

Peter Behrens

1868, Hamburg (Germany)
1940, Berlin (Germany)

• • • • • • • • • • • • • • • •

Modern design owes a great deal to this electric kettle. By combining the possibilities of three basic forms, three materials and three surface finishes, it was theoretically capable of being produced in 80 versions (though only 30 were in fact available) – a mix of standardisation and personalisation that is returning to the forefront in design today. The kettle derives from the ideas of the Deutscher Werkbund, a design association whose goal was to raise the technical and aesthetic standard of German products, until then considered inferior. Unlike the English Arts and Crafts movement, the Deutscher Werkbund did not reject industrial production, but sought rather to improve it. One of the co-founders of the association in 1907,

Peter Behrens was also the design consultant to AEG [the Allgemeine Elektricitäts Gesellschaft or "General Electrical Company"], for which he created this kettle. A painter by training, he also designed the company's logo, unchanged since then, and even buildings: built in Berlin in 1909, his turbine factory is a masterpiece of 20th-century architecture. Behrens was thus responsible for inventing the notions of brand identity and holistic design still current today, as indeed is the association between Germany and quality manufacturing that he did so much to promote • **XJ**

← **1922**

Office Lamp, No 211
Manufacturer: Ravel (France)
Metal (nickel-plated)
Lamp
50 cm (h)
Reflector
15 cm (h) x 20 cm (∅),
1.3 kg (weight)
Purchase, 2006 - AM 2006-1-46

Atelier Gras

· ·

While he had been designing lighting equipment since 1905, it was on 13 October 1921 that engineer Bernard-Albin Gras patented an articulated lamp for use at work. In designing his first models, he had sought above all to improve on existing office lamps, notably fixed arm types, while incorporating electricity into the design. His concerns were ease of use and the efficiency of the light source. A symbol of functionality, this piece ignores conventional aesthetic considerations in a quest for usability and manipulability. Each of the elements forms an integral part of a whole reduced to its functions – whether hanging or wall-mounted light, standard lamp or office lamp. Gras lighting appeared everywhere in factories, workshops, architects' offices, research laboratories, public institutions. The strength of the Gras lamps lay in the fact that form, as well as size and colour, could be matched to the environment. Given this, architects and designers of the rank of Le Corbusier, Robert Mallet-Stevens and Eileen Gray wasted no time in providing themselves with this discreet but efficient articulated lamp, and it is no surprise that Hans Richter should have taken it as a symbol of the new functionalism in his film *Die Neue Wohnung* [The Modern Home] of 1930 • **CP**

Pierre Chareau

1883, Bordeaux (France)
1950, New York (United States)

• • • • • • • • • • • • • • •

Known as the *Grande Religieuse*
[Large Nun], no doubt on account of its
general appearance, this floor lamp was
designed by Pierre Chareau and made
by master metal worker Louis Dalbet.
It was in 1923 that Chareau discovered
Dalbet's skills and developed the use
of metal in his own work. Whether
in furniture, interior design or
architecture, Chareau's work is
characterised by formal simplicity.
From 1923 on, he designed numerous
light-fittings in metal and alabaster, a
translucent stone somewhat resembling
marble. Dalbet produced the fixing
brackets and the mounts, and cut and
fitted the alabaster. Cut into simple
geometric forms – quarter-circles,
triangles or rectangles – this was
positioned in front of the bulbs, in pairs
or fans. The multidirectional play
of light itself made any other form
of decoration unnecessary.
The Centre's lamp is constructed from
two modular forms, the triangle and
the cone. The metal base is an indented
cone of wrought sheet iron curled and
folded, the horizontal line of the
bottom end being fixed by standing it
in water. The four overlapping triangles
of alabaster are fixed to it by mobile
corner mounts of brass. This metal base
appears to have been a prototype; other
models in this series were produced in
wood, in three sizes: reading lamp, table
lamp, and floor lamp. Some were fitted
with traditional shades • **AMZ**

⊻ **1923**

**Floor Lamp, known
as the "Grande
Religieuse"**
Maker: Louis Dalbet, master
metalworker (France)
Iron, alabaster and brass
171 x 45 x 55 cm
Purchase, supported by
the Scaler Foundation, 1995
AM 1995-1-46

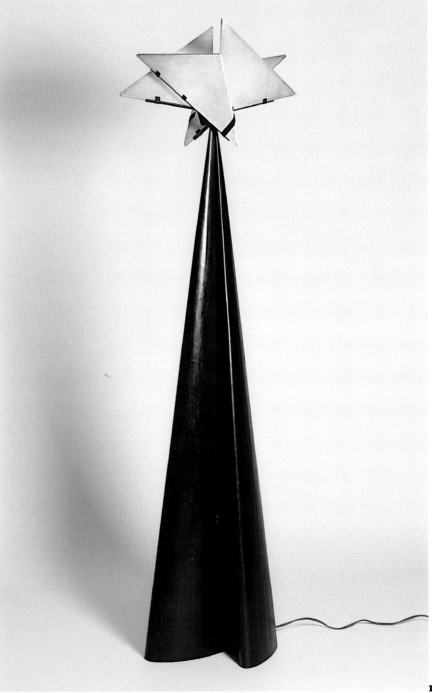

⬆ 1923

"Staatliches Bauhaus" Poster

Printer: Reineck & Klein
(Germany)
Lithograph and paper strip
68.3 x 48 cm (without frame)
77.6 x 56.9 x 4.2 cm (with frame)
Purchase, 1999 - AM 1999-1-16

Joost Schmidt

1893, Wunstorf (Germany)
1948, Nuremberg (Germany)

• • • • • • • • • • • • • • • • • • • •

A painter by training, Joost Schmidt
joined the Bauhaus at Weimar at
the end of the First World War. In
the summer of 1923, its director Walter
Gropius organised a vast exhibition
of work by students and teachers, in
the hope of obtaining financial support
from the Land government.

It fell to Joost Schmidt to produce the
poster. His design follows the principles
of form propounded by Oskar
Schlemmer, while the lettering stands
in the line of Herbert Bayer's
typographical investigations. The
orthogonal, three-colour composition
(in black, white and red) combines
straight edges with circles, half-circles
and quarter-circles, and in the one full
circle he places the stylised face
conceived by Schlemmer as the
Bauhaus logo in 1922.

It is through the form, size and colour
of the lettering that Schmidt brings
organization and rhythm to the flat
composition. To accentuate the clarity
and legibility of the message, he swings
the entire motif through 45 degrees, the
whole composition being thus
articulated about a strong and dynamic
diagonal axis.

In accord with its purpose as a
communication, the poster establishes
innovative visual relations between
content and form, in a manner indebted
to the New Typography • **CP**

Josef Hartwig

1880, Munich (Germany)
1956, Frankfurt-am-Main (Federal Republic of Germany)

● ● ● ● ● ● ● ● ● ● ● ● ● ● ● ● ● ●

Trained as a stone carver, Josef Hartwig was appointed supervising master craftsman of the Bauhaus sculpture workshop in 1921. Around 1923, inspired by an idea by De Stijl artist Vilmos Huszár, he created a radically new chess set, the pieces taking basic geometrical forms of Constructivist inspiration that echo the way each moves across the board.

The basic element, a solid cube, is used for castles and pawns, which move in straight lines. A cube surmounted by an oblique cross stands for the bishop and its back and forth along the diagonals. A combination of four cubes renders the right-angle turn of the knight. A small cube superimposed at 45° upon the basic cube represents the king, which moves along both perpendicular and diagonal axes, while a cube surmounted by a sphere suggests the mobility of the queen. In certain variations on this last piece, the cubic base is replaced by a cylinder or polygon. The set would be produced in three versions, the first being hand-made in stained limewood. The painter Joost Schmidt, later master of the sculpture and printing workshops at the Bauhaus, was responsible for the graphic design of the cardboard box. As in the exhibition poster he made the same year, he here applies the principles of form, colour and typography then being promoted by the Bauhaus • CP

⬇ 1923-1924

Chess Set
Pearwood, cardboard and paper
5.5 x 12.5 x 12.5 cm
Gift of the Clarence Westbury Foundation (Houston, United States), 1999 - AM 1998-1-23

Marcel Breuer

1902, Pécs (Austria-Hungary, today Hungary)
1981, New York (United States)

● ● ● ● ● ● ● ● ● ● ● ● ● ● ● ● ● ●

We are in Germany, at the Bauhaus in Dessau. Founded by Walter Gropius in 1919, the school is the crucible of a new thinking about architecture and design, whose principles are functionalism and the fusion of art and craft. The Hungarian Marcel Breuer joined the Bauhaus as a student in 1920, at the age of 18. At 22, he led the cabinet-making workshop there. In 1925, he produced his first chair of tubular steel, the *B3* club chair, an airy revolution. His fellow teacher, the painter Wassily Kandinsky, who lived at the Bauhaus together with his wife Nina, commissioned dining room furniture from Breuer, requesting that the design should be based on the circle. He came up with a round table resting on eight fine steel tubes. Accompanying it were six chairs with circular seats on a frame and legs of wood. The backrest, also of wood, was mounted on metal tubes. In their general style, these chairs are inspired by the work of the Dutch designer Gerrit Rietveld, a member of De Stijl, more particularly in the painting of the ends of the legs in a lighter colour (yellow for Rietveld, white for Breuer). Kandinsky was very pleased with the end product, but Breuer thought it anecdotal. His later tubular steel furniture was indeed much more radical: it made him one of the great figures of Modernism, standing alongside Ludwig Mies Van der Rohe and Le Corbusier • XJ

◈ 1926

Dining Room Suite for Wassily Kandinsky

Commission

1 table
Wood and metal
75 cm (h) x 108 cm (ø)
Bequest of Mrs. Nina Kandinsky (Neuilly-sur-Seine, France), 1981
AM 81-65-917 (1)

6 chairs
Wood and textile
95 x 50 x 55 cm (each)

Bequest of Mrs. Nina Kandinsky (Neuilly-sur-Seine, France), 1981
AM 81-65-917 (2 à 7)

**Sphère No 4/6
Lamp**
Manufacturer: Décoration
Intérieure Moderne (in
collaboration with René
Koechlin)
Aluminium and ebonite
30 cm (h) x 25 cm (ø)
Purchase, 1994 - AM 1994-1-424

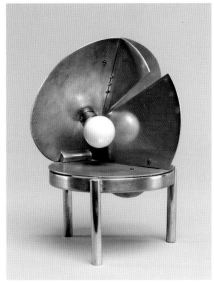

Jacques
Le Chevallier

1896, Paris (France)
1987, Fontenay-aux-Roses (France)

• • • • • • • • • • • • • • • •

Jacques Le Chevallier's *Sphère No 4/6*
lamp is a landmark in French lighting
design. First sketched in early winter
1926, it was produced in 1927 and shown
at the Salon d'Automne of 1928.
Something of a sideline for this master
glassmaker, his work with lights
produced a series of some twenty
models, designed in collaboration with

engineer René Koechlin between 1926
and 1930.
Breaking with the prevailing codes of
the time, Le Chevallier adopted for
Sphère No 4/6 a resolutely innovative
approach. Unlike his contemporaries,
who wanted light to fill space, he
preferred to direct it. His arrangements
of metal plates contain the light, to
project it in a cunningly contrived play
of luminosity. A movable metal sphere
rendered in intersecting planes, the
lamp rests on a circular tripod.
Constructed of aluminium, Duralumin
and ebonite, beneath its sculptural
appearance the lamp hides a skilful
combination of industrial techniques

and craft skills.
The lamp was first produced and
distributed by DIM (Décoration
Intérieure Moderne). In 1930, the
production contract was taken over by
master glassmaker Louis Barillet, a
collaborator of Le Chevallier's between
1920 and 1945, who developed
production in collaboration with René
Koechlin and a Parisian
manufacturer • **CP**

Robert Mallet-Stevens

1886, Paris (France)
1945, Paris (France)

• • • • • • • • • • • • • • • • • • •

In 1923, Charles and Marie-Laure de Noailles asked Robert Mallet-Stevens to build a villa for them at Hyères. He had until then essentially designed furniture and interiors, and this was his first architectural project, offering him an opportunity to put into practice his thoughts about the interdependence of architecture and the decorative arts. Modest at first, the programme became more ambitious as construction proceeded. By 1932, it occupied more 2,000 m² and boasted some sixty rooms together with sports facilities. To decorate and furnish the interiors, already animated by the play of light

and the abstraction of volumes, Mallet-Stevens turned to Djo-Bourgeois, Pierre Chareau, Francis Jourdain, Theo Van Doesburg, Marcel Breuer and Sybold Van Ravesteyn. He himself designed some of the furniture, including these garden chairs with their green-painted tubular steel frames and seats of beige cotton canvas, made for the terrace of the swimming pool, completed in 1927. Rationalism and hygienic concerns led to a characteristic geometrical simplification. Although suitable for series production, they were only ever produced in small numbers by the Établissements D'Autremont. Mallet-Stevens designed a second such light armchair, more compact, with a simplified metal frame. Several of these bridge chairs furnished the waiting room to his office at his Paris house • **AMZ**

⊻ [1927]

Chair
Manufacturer: Établissements D'Autremont et Cie (France)
Tubular steel and cotton canvas
92 x 63 x 92 cm
Purchase, 1995 - AM 1995-1-51

**Desk for Robert
Mallet-Stevens**
Wood and steel
Desk
66 x 103 x 162 cm
Stool
36 x 50 x 30 cm

Purchase, supported by the
Fonds du Patrimoine, 2004
AM 2004-1-20

Pierre Chareau

1883, Bordeaux (France)
1950, New York (United States)

• • • • • • • • • • • • • • • • • • •

In 1927, Robert Mallet-Stevens
commissioned from Pierre Chareau a
desk for the hall of his Paris house. The
two of them had already collaborated
on several projects. The wood and metal
desk that Chareau designed was made
at Ateliers Dalbet, who between 1927
and 1931 made some thirty desks, in
which metal plays a leading role.
Domestic heating systems, which
damage wood, new conceptions of
interior design and new standards of
hygiene all favoured the increasing use
of metal in furniture.
The desks were constructed on modular
principles, the black bands of the
wrought iron frame contrasting with
the polished wood of the work surfaces.

To meet clients' requirements, Chareau
could vary the shape of the desktop, the
number and placement of swing-out
tops, pedestal units, suspended drawer
units, etc. The Mallet-Stevens desk is of
black-stained beech on a frame of
nickel-plated metal (the only one of its
kind). This is made up, on one side, of
an inverted T-shaped piece of sheet
steel, on which is mounted a shelf,
while on the other, the legs and
crossbar rise above the desktop and its
suspended drawer to support an upper
shelf. Stability on the ground is ensured
by bending the end of the legs into feet.
As was often the case, the desk was
provided with a matching stool, whose
wooden seat is supported on a T-shaped
metal base. Chareau refuses decoration,
and leaves visible the hammered finish
of the metal: functional elements
become aesthetic • **AMZ**

← **1927**

M42 Rebil Chair
Manufacturer: Flambo (France)
Metal and fabric (velvet)
89 x 36 x 50 cm
Gift of Mr. Laurent Moos (Paris, France), 2008 - AM 2008-1-58

Henri Liber

A swivel chair with adjustable seat and back, the *M42* is the forerunner of the contemporary office chair. The engineer Henri Liber intended it for typists, who spent the whole day seated, but his chair, which won a prize at the Concours Lépine – the annual inventors' competition – would be widely used, even making its way into factories. Later versions would be padded. The "Rebil" range also included armchairs, desks and hanging file systems. From the Bauhaus to the mass production of the Ford Model T, the idea of rationalisation is all-pervasive in the early 20th century. Exploiting this principle, Henri Liber, who founded the famous Flambo company in 1919, specialised in furniture for the public sector, notably collaborating with René Herbst and Robert Mallet-Stevens. Purely ergonomic, his chair is the fruit of no theoretical approach, nor of any reflection on aesthetics, but it nonetheless displays an artless beauty. Like all industrial furniture, indeed, an interest in which has emerged over recent years • **XJ**

← **1927**

Extending Table
Maker: Jean Labadie, locksmith
Oak, linoleum, aluminium, steel and plywood
74 x 175 x 91 cm
Purchase, 1994 - AM 1994-1-302

Charlotte Perriand

1903, Paris (France)
1999, Paris (France)

It was in 1927 that Charlotte Perriand designed this table for her little apartment in Place Saint-Sulpice, Paris. She had that year already shown her *Bar sous le toit* at the Salon d'Automne, gaining herself a place with Le Corbusier and Pierre Jeanneret's firm as the partner responsible for interior design. Her dining room suite consisted of this *Extending Table* and swivel chairs. The table, which seats from 5 to 15, is notable for its top set into a sliding metal frame and consisting of wooden slats covered in black rubber. The top extends like a blind, the rollers being mounted on ball bearings in a case fixed to the wall at the other end. The legs of chromed steel tube that are pulled out to extend the table. Although then working for Le Corbusier and Jeanneret, in 1928 Perriand showed the table in her own name at the Salon des Artistes Décorateurs. Extremely well-received by the press, it was however never put into production. A luxury version, mounted on castors and operated by a handle, would be later manufactured by Thonet and presented at the first UAM exhibition at the Musée des Arts Décoratifs in 1930.
Remarkable for its innovative concept, Perriand's *Extending Table* also testifies to the advent of chrome-plated tube and with it the age of modern furniture • **MD**

**Rail-Mounted
Furniture**
Makers: Ébénisterie Besnard et
Flandrin and Établissements
D'Autremont (France)
Wood and metal
Purchase, 2005 - AM 2005-1-152

Francis
Jourdain

1876, Paris (France)
1958, Paris (France)

• • • • • • • • • • • • • • • • • •

In 1927, Robert Mallet-Stevens built a
house in Paris for the sculptors Jan and
Joël Martel. Comprising a studio and
three self-contained apartments, it is
informed by the rationalist principles
shared by all the designers involved in
the project: Gabriel Guévrékian, Jean
Prouvé, glassmaker Louis Barillet, and
the Martel brothers themselves. Jan
Martel's second-floor apartment fitted
out in early 1929, stands as a manifesto,
a year before the foundation of the
Union des Artistes Modernes. Designing
the bedroom himself, Jan Martel
commissioned a *Studio-Bar* from
Charlotte Perriand and confided the
living room to Francis Jourdain. At the

Ateliers Modernes, which he had
founded in 1912, Jourdain created
modular furniture through the
combination of simple, rational
elements, adaptable and
interchangeable, without any
ornament.
This *Rail-Mounted Furniture* for the
brothers Martel goes right around the
room. Suspended from the wall on two
parallel tracks, storage units can be
moved as required. Alongside them,
shelving, a divan, a desk with drop leaf
and side extension are all mounted on
the wall, leaving the floor clear and
easy to clean. A long mirror too takes
up the horizontal theme. The wood
furniture was made by cabinet-makers
Besnard et Flandrin of Paris, while
D'Autremont of Courbevoie was
responsible for the metal elements.
This functional ensemble echoes the
phrase of its designer Francis Jourdain:
"Unclutter. And if need be,
unfurnish" • **AMZ**

Bathroom Cupboard

Wood, aluminium, glass and cork
164 x 56 x 18 cm
Purchase, 1992 - AM 1992-1-6

Eileen Gray

1878, Enniscorthy (Ireland)
1976, Paris (France)

· ·

Eileen Gray designed this bathroom cabinet between 1927 and 1929, for the villa *E1027*, which she had just designed for herself at Roquebrune-Cap-Martin on the Côte d'Azur, assisted by architect Jean Badovici, founder of the journal *L'Architecture vivante*. In this building, almost a manifesto in itself, a diverse and multiple modernity finds expression in function and rationality, but also in aesthetics, fluidity, comfort and feeling. In 1930, the designer would show the plans and drawings for the house at the first exhibition of the Union des Artistes Modernes, of which she was a founding member. What she herself described as the "camping furniture" formed an integral element of the overall design: each room of the house is unique and designed together with its furniture, adapted to the space for which it is intended. So it is with this bathroom cabinet of painted wood, part-covered in sheet aluminium, which screens the washing area from the rest of the room. Its glass shelves, pivoting cork-lined drawers and compartments with fall flaps offer a well-considered range of storage possibilities, while the two asymmetric doors serve as mirrors. There are only two known examples of this piece, the second going into Gray's house Tempe a Pailla, at Castellar, also on the Mediterranean coast, completed in 1934 • **MTMR**

Eileen Gray

1878, Enniscorthy (Ireland)
1976, Paris (France)

• • • • • • • • • • • • • • • • • •

Between 1927 and 1929, Eileen Gray completed development of the *Transat* chair, intended for her villa *E1027* at Roquebrune-Cap-Martin, patenting it in 1930. She had shown the first drawings at the Salon des Artistes Décorateurs in 1924. While it embodies a very sober functionalism ("a machine for sitting in," said Le Corbusier) the craftsman-built *Transat* also exemplifies the art of Eileen Gray, all contrast and delicacy. Slung from a wooden frame, the supple, flexible seat of leather on latex foam is prolonged by a tilting headrest. It contrasts strongly with the rigorously geometrical construction of the frame, straight square sections of natural wood joined by chromed metal mounts. The Centre Pompidou's example comes from *E1027*. However, Eileen Gray made a number of versions of the chair: in painted wood, in different varnished woods, with seats of leather or natural linen canvas. She sold them at her own Galerie Jean Désert, in the Rue du Faubourg-Saint-Honoré, which served as a shop window for her work between 1922 and 1930. It was only in the late 1970s that the chair was again manufactured, by designer Andrée Putman's company Écart international • **MTMR**

⊘ 1927-1929

Transat Chair
Sycamore, nickel-plated steel and synthetic leather
79 x 56 x 98 cm
Purchase, 1992 - AM 1992-1-1

Le Corbusier, Charlotte Perriand, Pierre Jeanneret

Le Corbusier

(Charles-Édouard Jeanneret, known as)

1887, La Chaux-de-Fonds (Switzerland)
1965, Roquebrune-Cap-Martin (France)

Charlotte Perriand

1903, Paris (France)
1999, Paris (France)

Pierre Jeanneret

1896, Geneva (Switzerland)
1967, Geneva (Switzerland)

When she joined Le Corbusier and Jeanneret in 1927, Charlotte Perriand was made responsible for "storage, chairs and tables." This collaboration led to a series of metal furniture attributed to "Le Corbusier, Pierre Jeanneret, Charlotte Perriand." Influenced by Le Corbusier's architecture, Charlotte Perriand was innovative in her thinking about furniture and in her use of new materials such as metal and glass. All her furniture, notably including the *Chaise longue* and the *Grand Confort Chair*, was shown in "l'Équipement intérieur d'une habitation" ["Fittings for a Domestic Interior"] at the Salon d'Automne in 1929.

The prototype in the collection of the Centre Pompidou, which belonged to the designer herself, was created in 1928 and made by Jean Labadie. It is a cubic chair, nicknamed "the cushion basket" by its designer. The frame of blue-painted steel tube holds four removable, thick, feather-filled leather cushions that rest on a fabric-covered metal

⌃ 1928

Grand Confort Chair

Prototype
Steel, metal, leather and feather upholstery
67 x 97 x 70 cm
Donation in lieu, 2004
AM 2003-1-397

grille, serving for seat and backrest. The legs are longer at the front than at the back, tilting the chair slightly, making it more comfortable. Other prototypes were made, with variations in the legs and the colour of the frame. The *Grand Confort Chair* was produced by Heidi Weber in 1958, then put out by Cassina, under Le Corbusier's name, in 1964, and then, from 1987, under the name of all three designers, in versions large and small, available in leather or fabric • **MD 29**

1928

Tub Chair
Wood
68 x 53 x 50 cm
Purchase, 2004 - AM 2004-1-4

Giuseppe Pagano

(Giuseppe Pogatschnig, known as)

1896, Poreč (Austria-Hungary, today Croatia)
1945, Mauthausen (Austria)

. . . .

With its very simple lines, playing on the square and the circle, this tub chair reminds one a little of the *Barrel* chair designed by American architect Frank Lloyd Wright in 1904. Made of Buxus, a composite wood, it is one of the earliest examples of Italian rationalist design. It was commissioned by Turin businessman Riccardo Gualino, who promoted the emergence of a new industrial culture that he sought to develop with artists and architects. Among them was Giuseppe Pagano, who in 1928 built and furnished his company headquarters, the Palazzo Gualino, one of the first Italian examples of Modernist architecture. During the 1930s, Pagano's furniture took on lighter forms, often in bent wood, quite close to what was being produced at the same time by Finnish architect and designer Alvar Aalto. In 1931, he became joint editor of the magazine *La Casa bella*, and then organised a number of exhibitions, among them the Mostra Internazionale della Produzione in Serie, in 1940, which marked the birth of industrial design in his country. His writing and his work (architecture, furniture, railway carriages, systems of prefabrication…) would influence a whole generation of post-war Italian designers. Earlier a member of the Italian Fascist Party though an opponent of its monumental architecture, Pagano joined the Resistance in 1943, before being captured and dying in Mauthausen concentration camp in 1945 • **XJ**

. . . .

1929

Desk
Wood and metal
80 x 180.5 x 80.5 cm
Purchase, 2007 - AM 2007-1-24

Djo-Bourgeois

(Édouard-Joseph Bourgeois, known as)

1898, Bezons (France)
1937, Paris (France)

. . . .

With its three wooden tops supported on half-cylinders, this desk represents a transitional moment. It is no longer entirely Art Deco, as nothing about it suggests the French tradition of furniture; yet it cannot be ascribed to the Modern Movement of Le Corbusier and Charlotte Perriand, for although it is is extremely uncluttered, it is not the fruit of functionalist principles and it relies on no new technique, such as the use of steel tube. Its designer, the architect Édouard-Joseph Bourgeois, known as Djo-Bourgeois, would not join the Union des Artistes Modernes established in 1929, which brought together the whole avant-garde in architecture and design. Djo-Bourgeois devoted himself to interior design, gaining a name in particular for a dining room he conceived for the villa his friend Robert Mallet-Stevens designed for art patrons Charles and Marie-Laure de Noailles in 1924. The strong horizontals of this elegant desk indeed evoke the pavilion that Mallet-Stevens built for the Exposition Internationale des Arts Décoratifs in Paris in 1925. One can also see a suggestion of the Streamline, the aerodynamic style that emerged in the United States in 1930. Dying at 39, Djo-Bourgeois did not have the time to leave a lasting mark on his epoch, and remains one of the forgotten figures of French design • **XJ**

René Herbst

1891, Paris (France)
1982, Paris (France)

• • • • • • • • • • • • • • • • • •

René Herbst designed for the Salon d'Automne of 1926 this engineer's desk in bent sheet steel, which abandons all reference to tradition and heralds the production of the metal furniture typical of his work between 1927 and 1937. Easy to work, light, flexible and tough, steel lent itself to standardisation and encouraged emancipation from older aesthetic models. It became the favoured material of the interior designers of the Union des Artistes Modernes (UAM), of which Herbst was one of the founding members in 1930, alongside Robert Mallet-Stevens and Pierre Chareau. Like them, he was convinced of the need for the industrial production of quality furniture to meet the requirements of the general public.

The desk shown at the Salon d'Automne of 1929 consisted of a chrome-plated tubular steel frame supporting a table top that serves as the basic module to which storage units are added: a closed pedestal with a drawer at the top, and an open pedestal with shelves. This combination of series-produced elements in bent, welded and painted sheet steel, designed as compact and interchangeable units, is intended to produce a functional and adaptable piece that meets customer requirements. The tops are protected by bevelled plate glass. In 1930, Herbst provided a different version of this desk to the director of the Office Technique pour l'Utilisation de l'Acier (OTUA). Made completely of metal, this type of furniture proved to be heavy, difficult to move about, and costly, finding few buyers. Herbst would replace it with furniture combining wood and metal • **AMZ**

⚙ 1929

Desk
Sheet steel, steel, glass and metal
76 x 173 x 82 cm
Purchase, 1995 - AM 1995-1-45

Louis Sognot

1892, Paris (France)
1969, Paris (France)

Not greatly successful at the time, though widely copied since, in 1929 this barstool embodied the latest trends in French industrial design, such as characterised the early years of the Union des Artistes Modernes (UAM). A model of simplicity, it is one of the very first pieces by interior decorator and furniture designer Louis Sognot. Trained at the École Bernard Palissy, in 1919 he joined the Printemps department store's Primavera studio, working alongside its founder René Guilleré. In 1923, he began to show at the Salon des Artistes Décorateurs and the Salon d'Automne. In 1928, he formed a partnership with interior decorator Charlotte Alix, with whom he established the Bureau International des Arts Français. A member of the UAM from 1930 and a teacher at the École Boulle, he was, with Jacques Viénot, one of the founders of the Institut d'Esthétique Industrielle. When in the late 1920s he began to experiment with the use of metal and its associated techniques, he designed this stool, probably for a bar on a liner. It is remarkable for the general effect produced by the stylised S-shaped line of the steel tube, its symmetry suggesting reversibility. The circular wooden seat of the first model was padded and covered with moleskin fabric in a colour to match the surrounding scheme. Unlike the versions in chromed steel, this has the original finish of black paint on metal • **CP**

1929

Bar Stool
Prototype
Steel and imitation leather
Frame
77 cm (h) x 40 cm (Ø)
Cushion
32 cm (Ø)

Gift of *Mobilier et décoration*
(France), 2003 - AM 2003-1-48

⊕ **[1929-1930]**

Reclining Chair

Manufacturer: Ateliers Jean
Prouvé (France)
Sheet steel and plain weave
fabric
95 x 45 x 52 cm
Gift of the Prouvé family
(Nancy, France), 1993
AM 1993-1-757

Jean Prouvé

1901, Paris (France)
1984, Nancy (France)

• • • • • • • • • • • • • • • • • •

Then a master metalworker, Jean
Prouvé experimented between 1929 and
1930 with his first prototype chairs:
intended for domestic use, they
illustrate his desire to produce
comfortable and solid pieces as
economically as possible.

When the Vosges industrialist Louis
Wittmann first commissioned him to
produce furniture for his chateau at
Rupt-sur-Moselle, he made him four
chairs with tilting seats, the leather
seat and back being stretched on a
frame of nickel-plated steel, and two
similar pieces for his own use. One of
these is now in the Centre Pompidou's
collection. The black-painted frame is
of pressed sheet steel, flattened tube
and welded round tube; the seat and
back are covered in red fabric. The seat
pivots on the underframe, the profiles
being wider where bending stresses are
greatest and narrower where they are
least. The structure thus makes visible
the mechanical forces in play.

Solutions could be transferred between
architecture and furniture. A variant
would be produced by Prouvé on the
marriage of one of his sisters, in 1930.
Although appearing in photograph in
the first catalogue of the Ateliers
Prouvé, this reclining chair never went
into series production. At the first
exhibition of the Union des Artistes
Modernes at the Pavillon de Marsan
in Paris, in 1930, Prouvé showed
it alongside the *Grand Repos*
armchair • **AMZ**

Émile Guillot

1892, Le Perreux-sur-Marne (France) ?
1960, Le Perreux-sur-Marne (France) ?

• • • • • • • • • • • • • • • • • • • •

This was one of the first tubular chairs to go into series production. The design is somewhat complex, the wooden seat resting on a horizontal tube at the back, while being fastened to the front tubes by brackets. Some versions were upholstered. Designed by architect Émile Guillot, this armchair was shown at the first exhibition of the Union des Artistes Modernes in 1930. One of the key products of the industrial age, used for piping, hospital beds, airframes and more, metal tube was first employed in domestic furniture at the Bauhaus in 1925, for Marcel Breuer's *B3* club chair. In 1928, Viennese manufacturers Thonet, until then known for mass-produced bentwood chairs, acquired the rights of the Standard-Möbel company, who manufactured Breuer's designs in Berlin, and embarked on the production of tubular furniture. It thus offered pieces (armchair, chaise longue) by Le Corbusier, Pierre Jeanneret and Charlotte Perriand. Thonet's French branch specialised in office furniture and called on Guillot's services, and this now-forgotten figure continued to design chairs, desks and filing cabinets until 1957 • **XJ**

❂ **1930**

B 257 Chair
Manufacturer: Thonet (Austria)
Chrome-plated steel and wood
81 x 52 x 58 cm
Gift of 15 Square de Vergennes
(Paris, France), 2004
AM 2004-1-19

André Lurçat

1894, Bruyères (France)
1970, Sceaux (France)

• • • • • • • • • • • • • • • • •

After first studying at Nancy, architect André Lurçat graduated from the École des Beaux-Arts in Paris in 1923. Better known for his buildings than his furniture, he began his career with the construction of eight houses with studios on the Villa Seurat private road, in Paris, one of these being for his brother, the painter Jean Lurçat. His lively interest in the design of interiors with integral furniture became evident at the Bomsel house and the Villa Hefferlin.

In the late 1920s, many of his interior designs were published in the *Répertoire du goût moderne*. Not long afterwards, he followed Le Corbusier and Charlotte Perriand, Béwé and Émile Guillot in establishing a long-term collaboration with furniture manufacturer Thonet. Turning to the use of bent metal tube, between 1930 and 1932, he designed more than a dozen pieces: chair, armchair, desk, pastry table and more. Simple in form, highly architectural in its geometrical lines, his furniture organised the physical division of functional space. An emblematic example of the rationalist tendency in European design, the Thonet *B 327* desk expresses the commitment to a new mode of industrial production that Lurçat, a member of the Union des Artistes Modernes, shared with many designers of the time. Illustrated in the Thonet Mundus catalogue of 1932, it testifies to this quest for an elemental functionalism • **CP**

⊘ **1930**

B 327 Desk
Manufacturer: Thonet (Germany)
Metal and wood veneer
73 x 175 x 105 cm
Shelf
43 x 103 cm
Drawer unit
86 x 36 x 36cm

Purchase, 2003 - AM 2003-1-332

← **1930**

Grand Repos Chair

Manufacturer: Ateliers Jean
Prouvé (France)
Sheet steel, horsehair and
canvas
94 x 68 x 108 cm
Purchase, supported by Pont-à-
Mousson SA, 1993 - AM 1993-1-756

Jean Prouvé

| 1901, Paris (France)
| 1984, Nancy (France)

• • • • • • • • • • • • • • • • • •

Designed by Jean Prouvé in 1930,
the *Grand Repos* is a reclining chair
that puts engineering at the service of
comfort. Combining the characteristics
of sheet steel with a self-adjusting
mechanism, it allows movement from
vertical to horizontal with a simple
shift of bodyweight. The first prototype
was shown the year it was designed at
the exhibition of the Union des Artistes
Modernes (UAM). The seat of folded
sheet steel is separate from the frame,
the base and arms on each side being
formed of a single piece of pressed
steel; it slides along notched tracks in
the armrests, controlled by springs in
the enclosed side-pieces, the load being
borne by the steel armrests.
The upholstery is covered in leather.
For a short series, the principle was
simplified, movement being controlled
by a single spring, with open side-pieces
leaving the mechanism visible, while
the horsehair padding was covered in
tent-cloth. Two examples, one of which
was kept by the designer, were
produced by the Ateliers Jean Prouvé.
Established in Nancy in 1931 for the
provision of "furniture, fixtures and
fittings," the firm was by then looking
for more profitable opportunities,
turning away from the household
sector, where the market was limited.
Prouvé thereafter devoted himself
to the series production of furniture
for institutions • **AMZ**

← **1930-1931**

Paimio Chair
Manufacturer: O.y. Huonekalu-ja
Rakennustyötehdas (Finland)
for Artek (Finland, after 1935)
Beech and birch plywood
63 x 60 x 87 cm
Purchase, 1993 - AM 1993-1-611

Alvar Aalto

1898, Kuortane (Finland)
1976, Helsinki (Finland)

• • • • • • • • • • • • • • •

After studying architecture at the Helsinki Polytechnic Institute, in 1918 Alvar Aalto embarked on research on the elastic properties of bent wood. In collaboration with Otto Korhonen, managing director of O.y. Huonekalu-ja Rakennustyötehdas, he developed a new process for bending wood and ply that allowed him to increase the resilience and thus the curvature of woods such as beech, birch and aspen. In 1930, he created this lounge chair for a sanatorium he was building in the Finnish town of Paimio. Intended to offer the patient the greatest ease in breathing, it is revolutionary in both form and design: light, movable and easy to look after. The S-shaped seat is in bent laminated birch; the springy scrolls at the ends rest on a looped frame of bent laminated beech. After a patent was obtained in 1931, the *Paimio* chair was produced in birch as *No 41*. To ensure the international distribution of his designs, in 1935 – together with his wife Aino Marsio and ex-collaborator Nils-Gustav Hahl and with the financial support of Maire Gullichsen – Aalto established a manufacturing company devoted to industrial design and modern art: Artek (art + technique). The example in the collection is one of the few not to have a crossbar joining the two back legs. It was shown in 1939 at the World's Fair in New York • **CP**

René Herbst

1891, Paris (France)
1982, Paris (France)

• • • • • • • • • • • • • • • • • • •

Dated 1930, this chair testifies to René
Herbst's constant research into the
comfort of his chairs, varying their
forms and combining different
materials with frames of steel tube.
Easy to work, suitable for mass
production and so less costly, steel tube
lends itself to every kind of
transformation: advantages that Herbst
would exploit for almost all his chairs.
For the seat and back he used rubber
shock cords used for chest expanders
and in car seats. Set close together,
these offered the comfort of a support
adapted to the body long before the
appearance of moulded plastics. They
were used in several different chairs,
armchairs and loungers. The first chair
of this type was shown at the Salon des
Décorateurs in 1927. At the Salon
d'Automne of 1929, Herbst set two such
armchairs on either side of a metal
desk. In the gym of the *Appartement du
jeune homme* on which he collaborated
with Charlotte Perriand, Louis Sognot,
Le Corbusier and Pierre Jeanneret for
the Brussels Exhibition of 1935, he
arranged beneath a fresco by Fernand
Léger a rowing machine, a punch ball
and other equipment, together with
a number of these chairs • **AMZ**

⬆ **1931**

Chair
Manufacturer: Établissements
René Herbst (France)
Steel and elastic rubber cord
82 x 44 x 47 cm
Accession, 1993 - AM 1993-1-817

Chair
Pencil and gouache on paper
26 x 16.5 cm
Purchase, 2003 - AM 2002-1-63

Robert Mallet-Stevens

1886, Paris (France)
1945, Paris (France)

This pencil drawing touched up with gouache signed by Robert Mallet-Stevens is for one of two models of chair attributed *ex post facto* to the architect. The first, manufactured by Tubor in 1931, is a metal chair in bent and welded steel tube. The seat may be of wood, perforated sheet steel, leather or fabric of various colours. As a supplier to the Paris Colonial Exhibition, railway companies and the Paris municipal administration, Tubor produced this in large numbers. The chair also featured in several interiors designed by the architect: the private houses in today's Rue Mallet-Stevens in Paris, his house for the Martel brothers, his studio for Louis Barillet, and the Villa Cavroix at Croix. Yet it appears under his name at no trade show nor any exhibition of the Union des Artistes Modernes.

The undated drawing is a sketch of a "plywood chair, with back of 2 metal slats. Painted tube, 49 F." This model was put into production by De Causse, at Tubor's old premises in Neuilly-sur-Seine, and later in Paris. Though the seat is different from that of the Tubor chair, the frame is exactly the same. Bent cold, welded and assembled with rivets, the chairs demanded little in the way of tooling. They are characterised by formal simplicity and by a significant new feature: stackability. Painted or chrome-plated, they were used at the Salon des Arts Ménagers, for whose design Mallet-Stevens was responsible from 1935 to 1939 • **AMZ**

Gerrit Rietveld

1888, Utrecht (Netherlands)
1964, Utrecht (Netherlands)

Having worked in his father's cabinet-making shop and trained as an architect, Gerrit Rietveld designed the *Red-Blue Chair* in 1918. The next year, he started his own firm and joined De Stijl. In 1924, he built the Schröder House, a building that stands as a Neo-Plasticist manifesto with its open plan, sliding partitions and functional use of colour. Four years later, Rietveld was one of the founding members of the Congrès Internationaux d'Architecture Moderne (Ciam).
Created in 1932, the *Zigzag* chair consists of three flat wooden elements arranged as a "Z" and crowned with a vertical backrest. Manufactured by Metz & Co. (Amsterdam), it is reinforced by wooden wedges at the two lower joints. It reflects the modernist project of a chair consisting of a single form, in which seat, back and frame are joined in a single continuous whole. In this respect, it is more radical than the cantilever chairs by Mart Stam and Marcel Breuer that preceded it. Furthermore, although Verner Panton rejected such a filiation, his own monobloc chair in a single monochrome material is formally very close to the *Zigzag*. The *Zigzag* armchair, its backrest with or without circular openings, is constructed in the same way, with the addition of armrests • **PT**

Zigzag Chair
Made for: Metz & Co
(Netherlands, 1935-1972), Cassina
(Italy, after 1972)
By : Gerard A. Van Groenekan,
cabinet-maker
Elmwood
88 x 53 x 77 cm
Gift of Mr. Jacques Boissonnas
(Paris, France), 1994
AM 1994-1-429

Chaise longue
Manufacturers: Embru (Switzerland),
Arnold (Germany), Stylclair
(France), A. L. Colombo (Italy)
Duralumin and wood
77 x 57 x 136 cm
Purchase, 1993 - AM 1993-1-605

Marcel Breuer

| 1902, Pécs (Austria-Hungary, today Hungary)
| 1981, New York (United States)

• • • • • • • • • • • • • • • • •

Trained at the Bauhaus, where he was
soon made head of the cabinet-making
workshop, Marcel Breuer later left
Dessau for Zurich, where he would live
from 1932 to 1934. This chaise longue is
one of a range of aluminium chairs
produced from 1932 onward by Embru
in Switzerland, Arnold in Germany,
Stylclair in France and A. L. Colombo in

Italy. Its curved lines are very different
from the geometrical look of Breuer's
earlier furniture in wood and then steel
tube. The originality of this chair, apart
from its ergonomics and its material,
lies in the way the aluminium strip
splits into two towards the back of each
floor runner, one part serving as base
and frame supporting the seat and
backrest, the second as a back leg that
becomes an armrest, contributing to
the rigidity of the whole. Shown at the
Concours International du Meilleur
Siège en Aluminium in Paris in 1933,
Breuer's range won the first prize,
awarded by two independent juries, one
of which was made up of industrialists,

the other including such figures as
Siegfried Giedion, Walter Gropius and
Le Corbusier. Yet it met with no success
among the public – perhaps on account
of the somewhat skeletal lack of
upholstery, though the seating is no
less comfortable for that, being to a
certain degree flexible – until it was
marketed as garden furniture. In 1935,
Breuer opened an architectural office
in London and designed a very similar
chair in ply and bent laminated wood
for the English company Isokon • **PT**

Eugène Beaudouin

1898, Paris (France)
1983, Paris (France)

Marcel Lods

1891, Paris (France)
1978, Paris (France)

• • • • • • • • • • • • • • • • • • • •

The *Chaise longue pour le repos* [Chaise Longue for Resting] was designed by architects Eugène Beaudouin and Marcel Lods, who in 1934-1935, at the request of Henri Sellier, mayor of Suresnes, built an open-air school for pre-tuberculous children on the southern slopes of Mont-Valérien. This was an occasion for experiment, where relations between inside and outside were inverted to ensure a maximum exposure to sunlight. Studies for the furniture were begun in 1934. Beaudouin and Lods adapted for outdoor use the models supplied to the schools of Suresnes Garden City by Ateliers Mécaniques La Gallia. For a first tender, Jean Prouvé collaborated with them in developing the aspects of lightness, modularity and comfort. He came up with several ideas, including one for a chaise longue with a frame of tubular sheet steel, but the Ateliers Prouvé did not take part in the final round of the competition. In 1935, the Surpil company was awarded the furniture contract for the primary school, and La Gallia that for the nursery school, as well as the contract for this camp bed, made, in accordance with the specifications laid down by Beaudouin and Lods, in polished Duralumin – a tough and corrosion-resistant aluminium alloy – and fitted with vulcanised rubber blocks for feet. Undyed cotton tarpaulin fabric is suspended from the frame by means of wooden rods that pass through sleeves at either end. The beds were set in the grounds and on the sun terraces to be used for the children's siesta • **AMZ**

▷ 1934-1935

Chaise longue pour le repos
Duralumin and cotton canvas

Structure
40 x 150 x 60 cm

Tube
3 cm (ø)

Gift of the Institut National Supérieur de Formation et de Recherche pour Jeunes Handicapés (Suresnes, France), 2006 - AM 2006-1-48

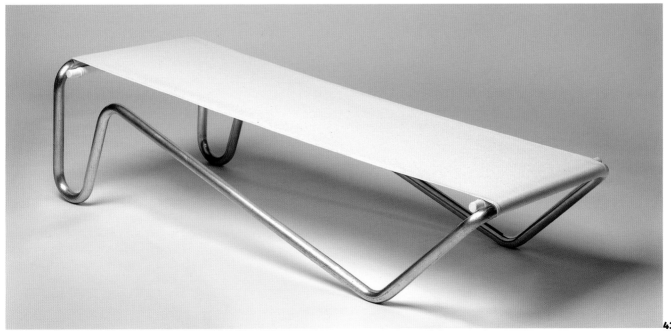

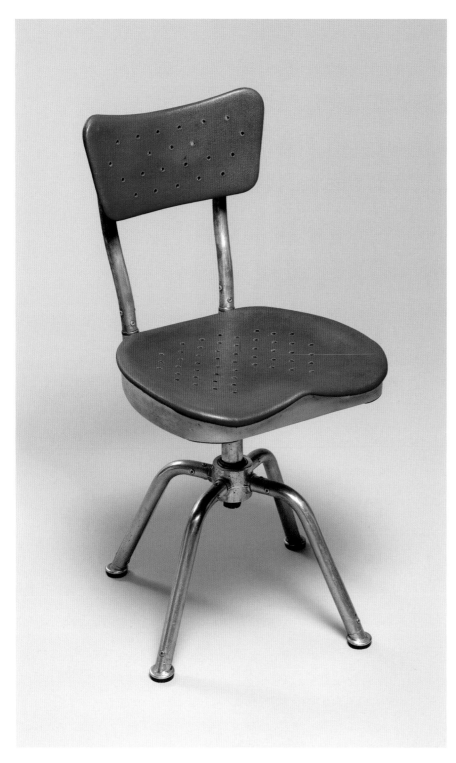

⬆ 1936-1938

Chair
Aluminium and leatherette
80 x 41 x 45 cm
Purchase, 2002 - AM 2002-1-16

Gio Ponti

1891, Milan (Italy)
1979, Milan (Italy

. . . .

Constructed of aluminium, this swivel
chair for typists is coeval with the
emergence of industrial design in Italy.
It was designed by Gio Ponti for the
Milan headquarters of chemical
manufacturers Montecatini; with its air
conditioning and state-of-the-art
telephone system, this was a true
celebration of the power of industry.
In a spirit of total design, the architect
took responsibility for everything: the
building itself, with its smooth marble
walls, the furniture, the sanitary
installations, even the clocks and the
doorknobs. There were seven kinds of
chairs, differentiated by use and by
rank of occupant. Functional in their
lines yet refined in such details as their
red upholstery, these pieces are less
well known than Ponti's domestic
furniture, in which the designer often
showed a degree of humour and
whimsy. With his measured modernism,
happy to make classical allusions, and
his multiple talents, Ponti was a key
figure in Italian architecture and
design. A proponent of rationalism, in
1928 he founded the magazine *Domus*,
still published today, editing it until his
death. Poet, ceramicist, artistic director
of publishers Fontana Arte, he helped
launch the Milan Triennale in 1933. To
him, we owe not only the *Pavoni*
espresso machine, which conquered
post-War Italy, and the *Superleggera*
chair of 1957, still manufactured by
Cassina, but also the first Italian
skyscraper, the Pirelli Tower that has
dominated Milan since 1958 • **XJ**

René Coulon

1908, Paris (France)
1997, Paris (France)

● ● ● ● ● ● ● ● ● ● ● ● ● ● ● ● ● ● ●

The work of architect René-André Coulon came to attention in 1937 at the Exposition Internationale des Arts et Techniques, where he worked on the Hygiene Pavilion alongside Robert Mallet-Stevens, and, more substantially, on the Saint-Gobain Pavilion, built in collaboration with architect and interior designer Jacques Adnet. A technical feat and a manifesto of Modernism, this building of glass and steel on concrete foundations is innovative through and through. From façade to furniture, the glassmaker's products were used in every conceivable form: translucent bricks, glass paving, glass panels, bent plate glass…

The *Radiaver*, an electric radiator as famous as it is unusual, makes use of the tougher tempered glass. Supported by two tubular metal mounts, two tempered glass plates enclosing a metal heating element slide into a pressed glass base of granular pattern. Manufactured by Saint-Gobain for Paris mirror merchants Hagnauer, the heater did not have the success expected, despite the sober elegance of its design, the magic of transparency, the contrast of glass and metal. Yet it proved to be an exceptionally effective PR tool for Saint-Gobain, and on the basis of the experiments of 1937, Coulon established himself for many years as an indispensable partner in the company's research efforts • **CP**

⬆ **1937**

Radiaver Electric Heater

Manufacturer: Saint-Gobain (France)
Triplex glass and metal
51 x 43 x 13 cm
Purchase, 2002 - AM 2002-1-2

Hans Coray

1906, Zurich (Switzerland)
1991, Zurich (Switzerland)

Self-taught, Hans Coray embarked on furniture design in 1930. The career of his *Landi* chair, designed in 1938, began the following year when it won the design competition for an outdoor chair for the Swiss National Exhibition of 1939 organised by exhibition architect Hans Fischli. It was the product of an effective collaboration between aluminium producers Rorschach and manufacturers Blattmann: in Switzerland on the eve of the Second World War, where aluminium was produced and exported, the metal was a favoured material. The *Landi* is made from an aluminium alloy specially treated to make it almost as tough as steel. Produced from a single sheet of aluminium cut and perforated in a single operation, the rigid shell is stiffened by the slight bulge around the holes. The chair quickly caught on with the public, who began using it indoors. It was therefore provided with four protective rubber feet: this is the case of the example in the Centre Pompidou's collection, which dates from 1962. With the difficulties, more particularly of stability, encountered by successive manufacturers, the number of holes has varied. Today, thanks to technical improvements, the *Landi* chair is again being manufactured in accordance with Hans Coray's initial design, which had 91 holes.

From the 1950s onward, Coray began to focus more on painting and sculpture in metal • **MTMR**

⬅ 1938

Landi Chair
Manufacturer: Zanotta Nova
Milanese (Italy)
Maker: Blattmann
Metallwarenfabrik (Switzerland)
Aluminium
75 x 49 x 60 cm
± 3 kg (weight)
Purchase, 1993 - AM 1993-1-660

Charlotte Perriand

1903, Paris (France)
1999, Paris (France)

• • • • • • • • • • • • • • • • • • •

While continuing to work on metal tube furniture – notably her *Bar sous le toit*, designed in 1927, and her *Salle à manger* of 1928 – Charlotte Perriand turned away from this to some degree to work with wood. With Le Corbusier and Jeanneret, she showed a rocking chair in wood and straw at the Brussels Exhibition of 1935, and then a set of wooden furniture at the Exposition Internationale des Arts et Techniques in Paris in 1937. She was then very far from the commitment to metal that characterised her article "Wood or Metal?" published in *The Studio* in 1929. A lover of the Alps, she drew on the region's architecture, its traditional materials and its forms, adapting their spirit to modern needs.

In 1937, she left Le Corbusier's firm, and the following year she designed for her studio flat in Montparnasse this first, asymmetrical, six-sided *Table en forme*. Produced by Charpentiers de Paris, it is made from the deal timbers salvaged by Pierre Jeanneret after the closure of the Pavillon des Temps Nouveaux at the 1937 Exhibition. The three legs are attached to the thick tabletop of natural wood by mortise-and-tenon joints. Adapted to the layout of the room, it can seat six or seven without taking up too much space. Nine more of these tables were made after the Second World War • **MD**

⬆ 1938

Table en forme
Maker: Les Charpentiers de Paris (France)
Deal
69 x 183 x 125 cm
6.5 cm (depth of top)
Purchase, 1995 - AM 1995-1-48

Bruno Mathsson

1907, Värnamo (Sweden)
1988, Värnamo (Sweden)

• • • • • • • • • • • • • • • •

Offspring of a line of cabinet-makers, Bruno Mathsson was an architect and self-taught designer. In 1931, commissioned to design furniture for the Värnamo hospital, he experimented for the first time with bent laminated wood. Inspired by the theories of biologist Are Waerland, who promoted natural living, he created his first chairs with ergonomic interwoven webbing. In 1936, at his exhibition at the Röhsska Design Museet, Göteborg, he showed chairs with flax webbing and with straps of leather, sheepskin, cowhide and deer hide. He developed a seating typology of three categories: lounge chairs, easy chairs and working chairs.

Invited by the Swedish Society of Industrial Design to exhibit at the Swedish Pavilion at the Exposition Internationale des Arts et Techniques in Paris in 1939, he was commissioned two years later by Edgar Kaufmann Jr. to design bentwood chairs for the new MoMA. Internationally recognized and exhibited, in 1943 he created one of his most important pieces, the *Pernilla* lounge chair, which exploits the traditional idea of warp and weft and testifies to an exceptional skill in wood technique. Comprising a seat with footrest it is made of natural materials in plain colours. Given the shortage of textile fibre, the interwoven straps were of twisted Kraft paper. Bruno Mathsson named the chair for Pernilla Tunberger, a journalist on the daily newspaper *Dagens Nyheter* who had interviewed him on matters of comfort and hygiene • **OR**

⊘ **1943**

Pernilla Chaise Longue

Beech and woven paper
Chaise longue
90 x 110 x 70 cm
Footrest
40 x 50 x 70 cm

Gift of Galerie Christine Diegoni-Zyman (Paris, France), 2009 - AM 2009-1-82

Eero Saarinen

1910, Kirkkonummi (Finland)
1961, Ann Arbor (United States)

• • • • • • • • • • • • • • • • • • •

Trained in sculpture at the Académie de la Grande Chaumière in France, Eero Saarinen graduated in architecture from Yale in 1934. He afterwards worked with his father, the well known architect Eliel Saarinen, president of the Cranbook Academy of Art. Invited to teach there, he got to know designer Charles Eames, with whom he investigated organic design, more particularly the use of moulded plywood shells. In 1940, the two designers won first prize in the competition "Organic Design in Home Furnishings" organised by MoMA, New York. The end of the war saw an end to

their collaboration, and Saarinen teamed up with a New Jersey boat-builder to produce a light and comfortable armchair. Using polyester resin reinforced with glass fibre and wood shavings he created a moulded shell that was then lined with latex foam and covered in polyester fabric. The whole was supported on a frame of slender steel tube and fitted with removable cushions. Put on the market by Knoll Associates in 1948, the chair revolutionised expectations, answering precisely (as suggested by its name) to the new principles of relaxation and well-being. A year later, Saarinen would complement the chair with an ottoman and a two-seater sofa • **CP**

⚇ 1946-1947

Womb Chair
Manufacturer: Knoll Associates (United States)

Chair
Fibreglass-reinforced polyester, steel, latex foam and polyester fabric
90 x 100 x 88 cm
Gift of Mr. Alexander von Vegesack (Weil am Rhein, Germany), 1993 - AM 1993-1-656

Footstool
Plywood, latex foam, steel and polyester fabric
40 x 63 x 55 cm
Gift of Mr. Alexander von Vegesack (Weil am Rhein, Germany), 1993 - AM 1993-1-657

Charles Eames

1907, Saint Louis (United States)
1978, Saint Louis (United States)

Ray Eames
(Bernice Alexandra Kaiser, known as)

1912, Sacramento (United States)
1988, Los Angeles (United States)

Between 1941 and 1978, American designers Charles and Ray Eames developed some twenty different chairs, each reflecting their ambition to create a mass-market industrial product in simple forms suited to the essential requirements of the body. While early experiments with moulding plywood or aluminium sheet proved unsatisfactory, fibreglass-reinforced polyester resin opened up a wide field of formal possibilities. This man-made material, used notably in airplane construction, had not before been used for furniture. Suitable for moulding, tough, flexible and pleasant to the touch, it was cheap and suited to industrial production. In 1946, furniture manufacturer Herman Miller gained the exclusive right to produce and distribute the first ever chairs in man-made materials, designed by Charles and Ray Eames. Together with them he established unequalled standards of production. The *Paw Chair* is one of a series of eight chairs formed of a single shell moulded to the contours of the body. With or without armrests, these chairs and armchairs in bright self-colours stand on legs that vary in form and material with the model and the use, domestic or occupational, for which it is intended. They are also sometimes mounted on rockers. The *Paw Chair* has wooden legs braced with steel rods. It differs from the similar *Daw Chair* by the addition of a swivel • **AMZ**

➔ 1948

Paw Chair

Maker: Zenith Plastics (United States)
for manufacturer Herman Miller (United States)
Fibreglass-reinforced polyester, wood and steel wire
78 x 62 x 60 cm
Gift of M. Alexander von Vegesack (Weil am Rhein, Germany), 1993 - AM 1993-1-640

Bic

Founded in 1945, the company took the name "Bic" in 1953

In the middle of the last century, the business of writing was radically transformed with the shift from pen and nib, with its contrast of swells and hairlines, to the uniform line of the ballpoint pen. It was a Hungarian journalist, László Bíró, tired of the inconveniences of the fountain pen, who in 1943 developed a system that borrowed a technique from printing, with a ball-bearing controlling the delivery, as required, of ink held in a tube above. In 1950, with the French economy in the throes of post-War modernisation, and with ballpoint pens already available, at a price, in many other countries, the Frenchman Marcel Bich bought Bíró's patent. He used a process that allowed the mass production of a plastic pen, available in four colours (black, blue, red and green). Light, transparent, functional, cheap and of good quality, he baptised it the "Bic," a homophone of his own name, the name being taken by the company too in 1953. Since then, millions of *Bic Cristal* ballpoint pens have been sold across the world. If the design remains unchanged – except for the hole in the cap introduced for child safety reasons – the ink and the ballpoint are subject to constant technical innovation. The four pens in the Centre Pompidou's collection represent the first model, designed by the Décolletage Plastique design team • **MTMR**

→ **1950**

Bic Cristal
Manufacturer: Bic (France)
Polystyrene, polypropylene
Ballpoint of tungsten carbide
15 cm (h) x 6 mm (ø)
2 km (writing length)
Gift of Bic (Clichy, France), 2006
AM 2006-1-37

Carlo Mollino

1905, Turin (Italy)
1973, Turin (Italy)

• • • • • • • • • • • • • • • • • • •

This desk is a one-off, and one of Carlo Mollino's most important pieces. Intended in 1950 for a never-realised refurbishment of the Singer shop in Turin, it was bought that year by the designer's friend Mario Damonte, for the Istituto di Cooperazione Sanitaria medical centre in the same city. Mollino used moulded plywood – not one of the new materials of the time, such as plastic – and avoided the simple assembly of differentiated units characteristic of the desk as a type. It is distinguished by its structure, literally load-bearing. This has something of sculpture, but sculpture of a new type, proper to the ingenious Carlo Mollino. Made from a single sheet of moulded ply, lightened with cut-outs, it expresses a precarious equilibrium between acute tensions even as it evinces an elegant fluidity of line. The drawer unit of solid wood on the right legs seems more suspended in a void than an element in the structural stability of the desk. The entire structure remains visible, thanks to the glass top. Without being figurative, its form recalling the body of a reclining woman seen from the back is characteristic of the sensual imagination of its non-conformist Italian designer, as keenly interested in eroticism and in photography as he was in car racing and aerial acrobatics • **MTMR**

⬇ 1950

Desk
One-off piece
Maker: Apelli & Varesio,
cabinet-makers (Italy)
Maple plywood, Triplex glass
and wood
78 x 205 x 94 cm
Purchase, 1998 - AM 1998-1-3

1950

**Dolphin Chaise
Longue**
Maker: Johannes Hansen,
cabinet-maker (Denmark)
Oak and brass
93 x 73 x 150 cm
20 kg (weight)
Purchase, supported by the
Clarence Westbury Foundation,
2007 - AM 2007-1-204

Hans J.
Wegner

1914, Tønder (Denmark)

2007, Copenhagen (Denmark)

• • • • • • • • • • • • • • • • •

Born in South Jutland, Denmark,
in 1914, Hans J. Wegner completed his
apprenticeship in cabinet-making
in 1931. He studied at the Copenhagen
School of Arts and Crafts from 1936
to 1938. His career was closely bound up
with the exhibitions organised annually
by the Copenhagen Cabinet-makers
Guild until 1966. Responding to the
industrial manufacture of reproduction
furniture, the Guild had decided
to collaborate with the furniture
department of the School, which led
to celebrated partnerships between

architects and cabinet-makers such
Hans Wegner's with cabinet-maker
Johannes Hansen. From 1940, Wegner
worked with Arne Jacobsen for the city
of Århus before establishing his own
firm in Gentofte in 1943.

The *Dolphin* chair was designed in 1950.
The refinement of the woven cane
and the precision in the treatment of
materials makes it a particularly light
and elegant piece. The tapering back
legs, prolongations of the armrests, give
the whole a very streamlined look, and
its name derives from its sculptural,
zoomorphic form.

The "Scandinavian Design for Living"
exhibition at Heal's, London, in 1951,
marked the first stage in the worldwide
recognition of Scandinavian design,
identified with a simple and authentic
way of life • **OR**

Marco Zanuso

1916, Milan (Italy)
2001, Milan (Italy)

• • • • • • • • • • • • • • • • • •

Responding to the success of the foam rubber discovered in the 1930s, in 1950 the Arflex division of Pirelli-Spasa commissioned Marco Zanuso to design a range of chairs for industrial mass production. Inspired by Pirelli's experiments with foam rubber for car seat upholstery, Zanuso had already created a first armchair with it in 1949: the *Antropus* chair, intended for short-run craft production. Simple in its organic yet functional form, the *Lady* chair represents the culmination of his researches into the properties of this new material. Designed for mass production, it consists of a wooden skeleton with rubberised webbing standing on metal legs, together with three independent elements: arms, seat and back. Designed according to ergonomic criteria, these were individually padded with moulded foam rubber of different densities and covered with fabric before being assembled.

Still in production today, the *Lady* chair exemplifies the role of the designer as it was understood by Marco Zanuso, which was to exploit technical innovations while having regard to both to formal concerns and the requirements of industrial production. He was awarded the Gold Medal at the Milan Triennale of 1951 • **MD**

⬆ **1951**

Lady Chair
Manufacturer: Arflex (Italy)
Metal, rubber and fabric
78 x 80 x 80 cm
Purchase, 1995 - AM 1995-1-5

Harry Bertoia

1915, San Lorenzo (Italy)
1978, Bally (United States)

• • • • • • • • • • • • • • • • •

During the three years (1943-1946) that he worked for Charles Eames's firm, Harry Bertoia was able to continue and develop his researches, on glue-laminated wood particularly, but disappointed in his professional relationship with Eames, he decided to leave. In designing the now classic *Diamond Chair* for Hans and Florence Knoll he must have called on his experience in steel-wire sculpture and jewellery (he had shown jewellery in New York in 1943). Created in 1952, this "jewel" used techniques similar to those used in both fields, and this is reflected in the results: elegance, subtlety, lightness and transparency. The chair is also both strong and springy. The diamond-shaped steel-wire seat has a square frame on which the pre-formed sections are individually welded in place. The whole rests on a base of bent steel rod, which might be said to act as a mount. Despite the relatively high cost of this complex, semi-artisanal style of production, Harry Bertoia developed with the help of Knoll technicians Richard Schultz and Don Petitt a series of chairs in pre-formed and welded steel wire still sold in good numbers today by Knoll International. *Diamond Chair* is the most significant contribution in the way of furniture by this eclectic designer • **MTMR**

⬆ **1952**

Diamond Chair
Manufacturer: Knoll Associates (United States)
Steel
70 x 112 x 80 cm
Gift of Mr. Alexander von Vegesack (Weil am Rhein, Germany), 1993 - AM 1993-1-655 **55**

⊘ **1952**

Wall-Mounted Bureau
Manufacturer: Établissements Dugarreau (France)
Traffolyte laminate and aluminium
59 x 152 x 46 cm
Purchase, 2005 - AM 2004-1-32

Janette Laverrière

| 1909, Lausanne (Switzerland)
| 2011, Paris (France)

• • • • • • • • • • • • • • • • • •

One of the very few women among the designers of her time, Janette Laverrière stood throughout her career for the spirit of freedom. Trained in drawing and decoration at Basel's Allgemeine Gewerbeschule, in 1931 she joined Jacques-Émile Ruhlmann's studio, where she met her future husband, Maurice Pré. Signed *M. J. Pré*, their earliest furniture won prizes at the "Home Idéal" and "Maison de Week-end" competitions. In 1937, they won a gold medal at the Paris Exhibition. The avant-gardist Janette Laverrière there showed a free-form platform that proposed a new way of life, close to the ground.

For the Salon des Artistes Décorateurs of 1952 she created a wall-mounted writing desk, supported by visible right-angle brackets. It consists of double-sided panels of Traffolyte, white outside, red inside, set in a frame of folded aluminium sheet. In using Traffolyte like this and leaving the aluminium structure visible, Janette Laverrière was being frank about the goal, which was to meet a need, simply and economically. An experienced colourist, she chose to present the desk against a background of horizontal coloured bands, establishing a remarkable dialogue of line and colour between the two-sided Traffolyte sheet, the linear aluminium structure and the painted stripes on the wall • **CP**

Poul Kjærholm

1929, Øster Vrå (Denmark)
1980, Hillerød (Denmark)

• • • • • • • • • • • • • • • • • • •

Poul Kjærholm studied cabinet-making at Copenhagen's School of Arts and Crafts. Between 1951 and 1967, he collaborated on many pieces of mass-produced furniture with manufacturer Ejvind Kold Christensen and then Fritz Hansen. His chairs are among the most significant examples of the modern Scandinavian furniture design of the 1950s, combining elegance and functionality. He was more particularly interested in the unusual combination of "cold" materials such as aluminium, wire or stainless steel with such "warm" materials as rope, leather, wood and cane. Developed with Chris Sørensen in 1953, the shell of this fireside chair is made of a single piece of moulded aluminium. The metal was injected through three holes in the mould, and the "gate marks" they left on unmoulding served as points of attachment for the steel legs. The three oblique legs are removable, facilitating shipping. This approach to the production process was intended to minimise investment costs. The shell's turned-back edge emphasized the supple tractability of the material, and would also help retain any later upholstery. The chair was shown in 1954 at the annual Copenhagen craft exhibition. This experimental model, produced only in small numbers, is a forerunner of the famous *PK9* chair of 1961 • **OR**

⊘ **1953-1954**

Fireside Chair

Manufacturer: Chris Sørensen (Denmark)
Aluminium and steel
63 x 63 x 67 cm
Purchase, 2004 - AM 2004-1-3

Serge Mouille

| 1922, Paris (France)
| 1988, Monthiers (France)

• • • • • • • • • • • • • • • • • • •

Graduating from the École des Arts Appliqués in 1941, Serge Mouille completed his apprenticeship as a silversmith with Gabriel Lacroix. Ten years later, he designed his first prototypes of lights in aluminium. With a technique distinctive to him that allowed him to express his talent to the full, he created a number of forms that would serve as a basis of an extensive range of reflectors, each of these being combined with a specific structure to produce floor lamps, wall lights, hanging lights, desk lamps and more. His artisanal style of production involved a series of stages: machine pressing, manual stretching or flattening, and trimming.

Inspired by natural forms, sometimes those of the female body, between 1952 and 1963 Mouille developed a range of some fifty pieces. From 1956, he showed at the Galerie Steph Simon in Paris, alongside Charlotte Perriand, Jean Nouvel, Isamu Noguchi and Jean Luce. In 1964, his rejection of industrial production in the face of growing demand led him to turn more towards teaching and research.

This wall-light with four hinged arms includes, on the upper arms, two reflectors called "lampadaire" [streetlight] and on the lower, two more called "casquette" [helmet]. Functional above all, it was made to order in answer to specific lighting problems. With its matt black exterior finish and white within, it established a discreet, delicate and graphic presence in its architectural context • **CP**

⌂ **1953-1958**

Wall Light
Manufacturer: Atelier de Serge Mouille (France)
Aluminium and metal
240 x 150 x 30 cm
Purchase, 1991 - AM 1992-1-62

Willy Guhl

1915, Stein am Rhein (Switzerland)
2004, Hemishofen (Switzerland)

• • • • • • • • • • • • • • • • • •

Trained at the Kunstgewerbeschule in Zurich – the school of applied arts where he was later a teacher and head of the department of interior design – the designer Willy Guhl set up his own firm in 1939. In the late 1940s, he did pioneering research in the field of plastic furniture, creating, for example, a chair with a shell of Scobalit, a fibreglass-reinforced epoxy resin. He thus developed a knowledge of moulding that he would exploit in this garden chair. Designed for Eternit, it is made of asbestos cement. Little used by designers, the material is here moulded in a single, continuous and resilient ribbon. The general appearance and conceptual economy of the chair derive from both minimalist aesthetics and ergonomic concerns. The chair is hollow beneath seat and back, which makes it light and confers on it a sculptural aspect, in that the void is central to modern sculpture. Slightly bowed, the lower part of the shell recalls a rockingchair. Though cheap to produce, the chair was taken out of production in the 1980s on account of the health risk it was found to represent. In the late 1990s, Guhl designed a new version, without asbestos, that has since become a classic • **PT**

⇩ 1954

Garden Chair
Manufacturer: Eternit
(Switzerland)
Asbestos cement
53 x 55 x 95 cm
Gift of the The Gallery
Mourmans (Maastricht,
Netherlands), 1996 - AM 1996-1-6

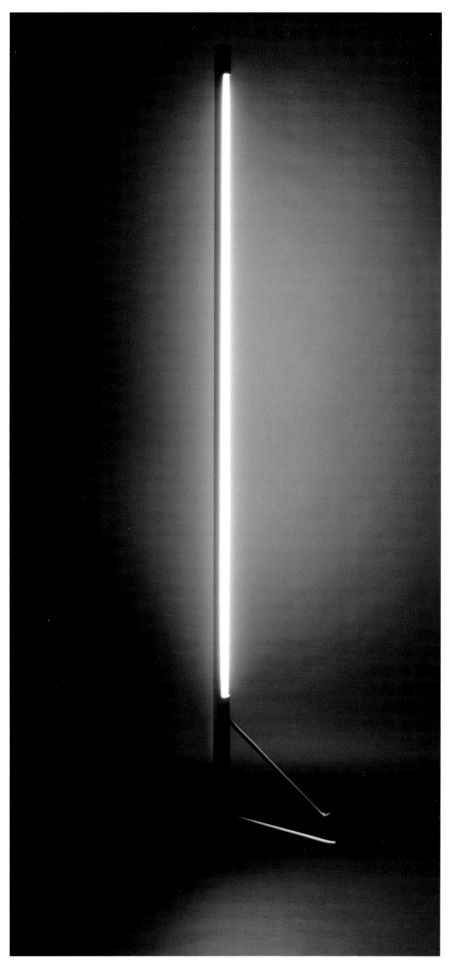

Floor Lamp (model 1063)
Manufacturer: Arteluce (Italy)
Steel
215 x 35 x 45 cm
Purchase, 2000 - AM 2000-1-10

Gino Sarfatti

1912, Venice (Italy)
1985, Gravellona Toce (Italy)

· · · · · · · · · · · · · · · · · · ·

In 1954, Gino Sarfatti designed for his manufacturing company Arteluce a floor lamp representative of his researches in lighting and of the formal solutions he tended to propose, dictated by study of the lightsource. Sarfatti had established Arteluce and opened a shop in Milan in 1939. He was part of the move to the industrialisation of Italian design promoted by Gio Ponti in his magazine *Domus*. After his light fixtures won the Compasso d'Oro in 1954 and 1955, he adopted simplified techniques that made mass production possible.

The key element in his designs is the bulb. Whether incandescent or fluorescent, it is what determines the form. Like Vittoriano Viganò and Achille and Pier Giacomo Castiglioni, Sarfatti sought to make it as visible as possible. He was a pioneer, indeed, in sometimes making it more or less the whole of the lamp, as in this lamp of 1954 (identified as product number 1063), structured around a fluorescent tube, until then little-used in domestic contexts. Standing upright, it is either clearly visible or partly hidden by the column of cut-out steel tube, depending on the angle of view and the way the lamp is positioned in the room. The light, projected or obscured by the column, plays with the shadow it creates. That same year, Sarfatti recycled the idea in designing a ceiling light consisting simply of two parallel fluorescent tubes • **AMZ**

Isamu Noguchi

1904, Los Angeles (United States)
1988, New York (United States)

• • • • • • • • • • • • • • • • • • • •

Conceived by Japanese-American designer Isamu Noguchi in 1955, as part of the *Akari* series of lamps [the name means "light" in Japanese], the *10A* lamp exemplifies the union of art and industrial design. More than a simple, functional light, it is intended as a luminous sculpture, an object in dialogue with space.
Noguchi's *Akari* lamps were commissioned by the municipality of Gifu. He chose to work within the long and familiar tradition of the *chochin* decorative paper lantern. Initially geometrical forms of eloquent simplicity, they become ever more complex light-objects in Noguchi's

hands. It would be wrong, however, to see this series of some hundred models, begun in 1951, as the fruit only of a formal exploration, for the designer wished above all to evoke through his lanterns a poetic world both fragile and ephemeral.
To symbolize this fragility, he chose *higo* bamboo and *washi* paper, made from the bark of the mulberry tree in the Mino region of Japan. The bamboo is used to create a ribbed structure that expands and collapses as required, while the translucence and silken touch of the paper soften an otherwise hard light. This bamboo-paper combination enters into dialogue with a third material – metal – with the addition of the airy tripod base. The light-object thus unfolds itself in space like calligraphy on a *kakemono*, a suspended scroll of silk or paper. It presents solid and void, black and white, light and shade • **CP**

⬆ **[1955]**

Lamps 10A and 3A
Manufacturer: Ozaki & Co (Japan)
Mulberry bark paper, bamboo and steel
Lamp 10A (1955)
123 cm (h) x 54 cm (ø)
Purchase, 1992 - AM 1992-1-295
Lamp 3A (1960/1970)
56 cm (h) x 30 cm (ø)
Purchase, 1992 - AM 1992-1-292

P40 Armchair
Manufacturer: Tecno (Italy)
Metal, steel, latex foam
and fabric
70 x 72 x 150 cm
Gift of Tecno (Milan, Italy), 1992
AM 1992-1-366

Osvaldo Borsani

1911, Varedo (Italy)
1985, Milan (Italy)

• • • • • • • • • • • • • • • • • • • •

The designer, architect and interior decorator Osvaldo Borsani started working in his family's furniture workshop at a young age. After gaining an architectural diploma at the Politecnico in Milan, he then turned to the interior design of offices and private homes. In this, traditional materials and skills were as important to him as technical innovations. His *E60* shelving (1946) testifies to a desire to rationalize storage systems that is not far – in spirit, at least – from American "good design." After the Second World War, as the pace of Italian industrialisation accelerated, he set up with his brother the Tecno furniture company (est. 1953), dedicated to mass production. Borsani designed armchairs, divans, tables and desks with distinct load-bearing structures or ingenious metal frames. Later, in 1966, he founded design magazine *Ottagono*. Halfway between armchair and chaise longue, the ergonomic *P40* chair has adjustable back, seat and footrest. As in the *D70* sofa bed, a great variety of positions are available to the user of the chair, which is still in production. The metal frame of the *P40* chair can be upholstered in fabric or leather, in a wide range of colours • **PT**

Wall Lamp
Manufacturer: Louis Poulsen
(Denmark)
Aluminium and brass
85 x 190.5 x 27.2 cm
Purchase, 2007 - AM 2007-1-202

Poul Henningsen

1894, Ordrup (Denmark)
1967, Copenhagen (Denmark)

• • • • • • • • • • • • • • • • • • •

Poul Henningsen was a left-wing Danish designer. In the late 1920s, he also turned to writing and founded the journal *Kritisk Revy* with Kaare Klint. He had very early on become interested in domestic and public lighting, developing mathematical and technical approaches to the problems of glare, shadow, the form of lighting structures and the distribution of light. His designs too were intended for a wide market, and in 1925, he began the mass production of lamps and light fittings with the Louis Poulsen company. After the Second World War, more than forty types of *PH* lights would be available. The spiral became a recurrent motif in his work from 1942 on.

This wall light in the Centre Pompidou's collection is one of twenty-four commissioned for the Scala cinema and concert hall in Aarhus in 1955. The ribbon of polished aluminium is painted on the inside to better reflect the light. In the 1980s, the cinema was renovated, and ten of these lights were disposed of, while fourteen remain in place, the double spirals forming an oblique line on the side walls of the raked auditorium. The building is today classified as a historic monument • **OR**

Le Corbusier

(Charles-Édouard Jeanneret, known as)

1887, La Chaux-de-Fonds (Switzerland)
1965, Roquebrune-Cap-Martin (France)

• • • • • • • • • • • • • •

In 1952, the Ateliers Le Corbusier had to fit out the kitchens for the 337 apartments of the Unité d'Habitation in Marseille, commissioned in 1945 by Raoul Dautry, Minister for Reconstruction and Town Planning. The project represented the culmination of the architect's researches in housing and urban planning. He made economical use of innovative construction techniques and standardised mass-produced elements, while the building itself was designed in accordance with the "Modulor," a system of proportions that would guarantee the harmony of the whole. In 1946, André Wogenscky developed the functional plan for the kitchen. Charlotte Perriand and Pierre Jeanneret were then responsible for the first phase of the design, which was later taken over by Wogenscky.

The kitchen is the central element of the apartments, which were designed as prefabricated cells. It opens onto the living room, being separated from it by a work surface; built-in are lighting, ventilation, waste disposal and a sink provided by Jean Prouvé. Like the rest of the apartment, it is provided with standardised storage cupboards, with sliding plywood or light metal doors and varied internal fittings. Two cupboards opening onto the "street-corridor" allowed for the direct delivery of foodstuffs and ice.

Three prototypes were developed before the kitchen was put into production. One was to be seen at the Salon des Arts Ménagers in Paris in 1950, as part of the model cell shown there • **AMZ**

⬇ **1955**

Atelier Le Corbusier Kitchen Type 1

Wood, aluminium and ceramic
Kitchen Units
224 x 216 x 129 cm
Partition
133 x 188 x 61 cm

Purchase, 2003 - AM 2003-1-25

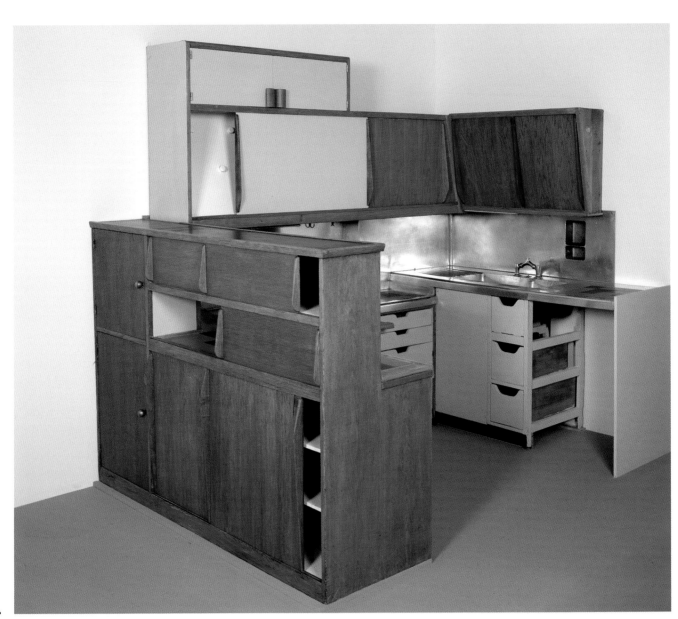

Fireside Chair
Steel, aluminium and wool
jersey
72 x 60 x 70 cm
Purchase, 2009 - AM 2009-1-36

Janine Abraham, Dirk Jan Rol

Janine Abraham

1929, Murat (France)
2005, Meudon (France)

Dirk Jan Rol

1929, Graft (Netherlands)

• • • • • • • • • • • • • • • • • • • •

The interior designer Janine Abraham worked successively for designers René-Jean Caillette and Maxime Old, before joining the firm of interior decorator Jacques Dumond in 1955. There she met her future husband, Dutch interior designer Dirk Jan Rol, with whom she would set up a firm of their own.

In 1956 they showed at the Salon des Artistes Décorateurs in Paris a chair that would win a silver medal at the Milan Triennale the following year. It had been designed in association with the Société de l'Aluminium Français, which in order to promote the use of its product supplied free aluminium to designers with innovative projects. Usually employed for office furniture, the designers used it here for a distinctively domestic fireside chair. Resting on a delicate frame of steel rod, two sheets of aluminium, each folded for strength, provided seat and backrest, both upholstered in foam and Knoll wool jersey. Two examples were hand-made, but no manufacturer would take on the risk of industrial production. They therefore designed another version in moulded plywood, made available in 1963 by Sièges Témoins.

Throughout their career, as here, Abraham and Rol created radically modern pieces, combining craft and industrial production • **CP**

⬆ **1956**

DAF Chair
from the "Swag Leg" series
Manufacturer: Herman Miller Inc.
(United States)
Steel and fibreglass reinforced
polyester
87 x 73 x 56 cm
Gift of M. Alexander von Vegesack
(Weil am Rhein, Germany), 1993
AM 1993-1-658

George Nelson

1908, Hartford (United States)
1986, New York (United States)

In 1956, the American designer George Nelson created the *DAF* chair as part of the "Swag Leg" series. As design director of the Herman Miller furniture company from 1944 to 1965, he was responsible for the manufacture of key pieces by Charles and Ray Eames and Isamu Noguchi.

In 1947, he set up his own design firm. For Herman Miller, he designed the "Swag Leg" series, named for the process called "swaging" responsible for the curved and tapered form that gave him the "sculptured legs" he wanted. The technical research was carried out by his collaborator Charles Pollock. Produced between 1954 and 1964, the chairs, desks and tables of this series are distinguished by the technique used in the production of the legs of tapered, curved and painted steel, easy and economical to produce and individually detachable to facilitate shipping. Seats or tops of varying materials were added to this common base.

The *DAF* chair is composed of two shells, giving a separate seat and back, and so a distinctive flex. They were made of moulded fibreglass-reinforced unsaturated polyester resin in a range of shades. The technique was innovative, but had already been used by the Eames. The moulded resin gave high quality pieces in very long runs. The seat is fixed to the legs by a rubber shock mount where they meet at the top • **AMZ**

Arne Jacobsen

1902, Copenhagen (Denmark)
1971, Copenhagen (Denmark)

Arne Jacobsen trained as a mason before studying architecture at the Royal Academy of Fine Arts in Copenhagen, graduating in 1928. A teacher between 1956 and 1965, he was with Poul Kjærholm and Verner Panton a leading representative of the Danish school of design, committed to mass production, the use of innovative materials and an international market. He won success in the early 1950s with his widely popular biomorphic chairs.

In 1956, he designed the SAS (Scandinavian Airlines System) Royal Hotel in Copenhagen: the horizontal element includes a vast lobby, restaurants and air terminal, while the 70-metre-high vertical slab houses 275 rooms. He also designed the furnishings, down to the door handles and the cutlery.

Designed in 1958 and manufactured by Fritz Hansen, the *Drop Chair* consists of a shell of moulded polyurethane, upholstered in glued foam rubber and leather. It stands in the line of Eero Saarinen's experiments with moulded plastic shells in the 1940s. Its four splayed legs in copper give it an unusual refinement. Forty such chairs stood in the hotel bar; others in the bedrooms were covered in solid-coloured fabric. In 1958, the Musée des Arts Décoratifs in Paris chose Jacobsen to represent Denmark at the "Formes Scandinaves" exhibition, the display taking as its theme the modern hotel room • **OR**

➔ **1958**

Drop Chair
Manufacturer: Fritz Hansen
(Denmark)
Leather and copper
70 x 45x 45 cm
Purchase, 2004 - AM 2004-1-23

Pierre Guariche

1926, Paris (France)
1995, Bandol (France)

● ● ● ● ● ● ● ● ● ● ● ● ● ● ● ● ●

Pierre Guariche designed this chaise longue in 1960, and it was manufactured that same year by Les Huchers Minvielle, among the keenest supporters of contemporary design. After establishing ARP (Atelier de recherche plastique) and there collaborating with Joseph-André Motte and Michel Mortier until 1957, Pierre Guariche would continue his researches on furniture, his goal being to use industrial mass production to produce quality furniture for the general public. Composed of one single piece, the wooden structure of this chaise longue is covered in foam rubber held in place by rubber straps. Replacing traditional padding, this new material adapted perfectly to the curved lines while offering great comfort. Covered in orange jersey, the chair swivels on a chrome-plated stainless steel base. Often compared to the chaise longue designed in 1929 by Le Corbusier, Pierre Jeanneret and Charlotte Perriand, it nonetheless heralds the new forms and the pleasure in colour of the 1960s, a decade of which Olivier Mourgue – with his famous *Djinn* chaise longue of 1964 – and Pierre Paulin – with his tongue-shaped stacking chair of 1966 – would be other notable representatives • **MD**

⊻ **1960**

Vallée Blanche Chaise Longue
Manufacturer: Les Huchers Minvielle (France)
Metal and wool jersey
75 x 75 x 157 cm
Purchase, 1992 - AM 1993-1-617

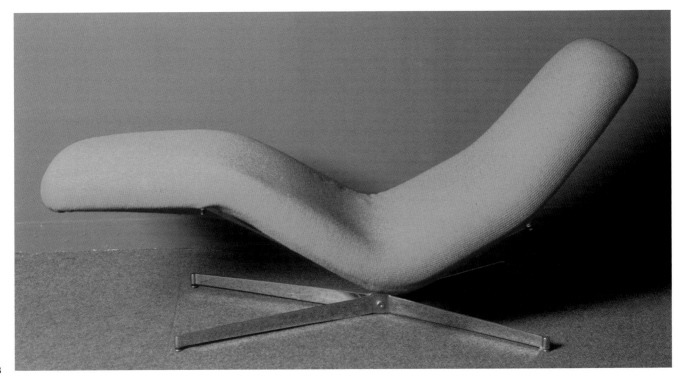

1962

Toio Floor Lamp
Manufacturer: Flos (Italy)
Steel and nickel-plated brass
163 x 22 x 20 cm
Gift of Strafor (Strasbourg,
France), 1997 - AM 1997-1-102

Achille Castiglioni, Pier Giacomo Castiglioni

Achille Castiglioni

1918, Milan (Italy)
2002, Milan (Italy)

Pier Giacomo Castiglioni

1913, Milan (Italy)
1968, Milan (Italy)

It was in 1962 that Achille Castiglioni and his brother Pier Giacomo designed the telescopic *Toio* floor lamp. Architects by training, the two brothers were emblematic figures of Italian design who contributed to their country's economic miracle in the 1950s and 1960s. Endowed with exuberant imagination and resistant to any functionalism, they offered a new approach to design, experimenting with great freedom. Drawing inspiration from existing objects in order to create others, they hijacked these forms from their original use, setting them in a new context and giving them an entirely different meaning. Like Marcel Duchamp, master of the ready-made, Achille and Pier Giacomo Castiglioni invented humorous and surprising assemblages that express their sense of play.

They thus assembled for this lamp a range of industrial components that have no intrinsic relation to each other: a 300-watt parabolic aluminised reflector lamp, a car headlight, is fixed to a nickel-plated brass stem; fishing rod rings guide the cable along the stem; a screw allows adjustment of the height; the transformer weights the base, part of which serves as a handle. The piece has been stripped of all superfluity, leaving only an essence behind. The *Toio* lamp remains an icon of Italian design, and is still manufactured by Flos • **MD**

⊘ **1962**

T1000 Radio
Manufacturer: Braun (Germany)
Plastic and aluminium
13.5 x 36 x 25 cm
Gift of Braun (Kronberg,
Germany), 1992 - AM 1993-1-555

Dieter Rams

I 1932, Wiesbaden (Germany)

Max Braun established his radio
manufacturing company in Frankfurt
in 1921. Thirty years later, his two sons
Artur and Erwin Braun planned to
radically extend the range of products.
In order to do this, in 1953 they
appointed as head of design Fritz
Eichler, a lecturer at the new and soon
to be famous Ulm School of Design. He
quickly laid down the five principles
that would make Braun's reputation:
functionality, quality, ergonomics,
aesthetics and innovation. In 1961,
Dieter Rams succeeded Eichler as head
of design, continuing in his
predecessor's footsteps with discreet
and sensitive designs: simple, balanced
and clearly organised.
The *T1000* radio that Rams designed in
1962 very rapidly gained a reputation
among specialists for its technical
sophistication. The latest model in
Braun's range of portable radios, it was
a highly sensitive receiver. Protected by
a drop-down cover, the control panel is
clearly and precisely organised. In the
original model, the loudspeaker stood
above the control panel. In the
production model, they are side by side.
Dieter Rams designed several other
versions of this radio, as well as a
matching portable TV, but they were
never manufactured and the *T1000*
radio remained the great success of the
period • **CP**

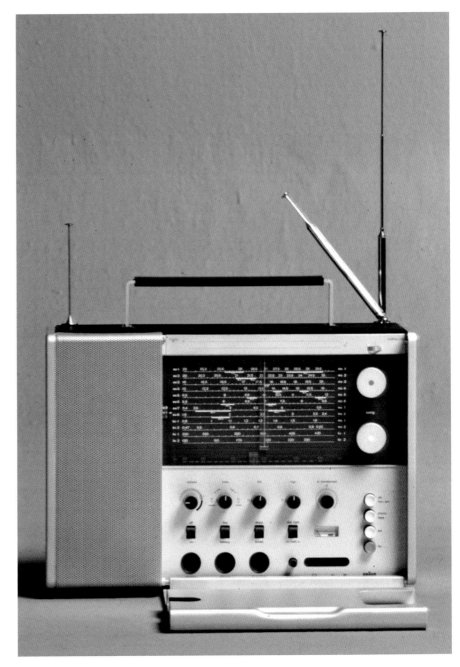

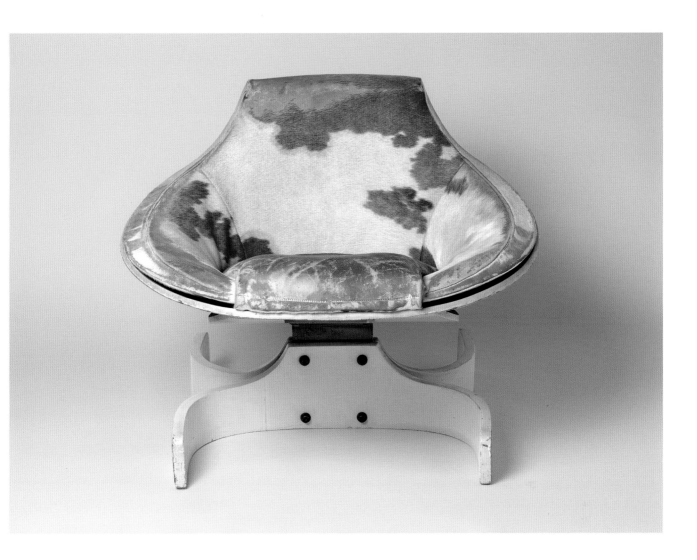

1963

La Sella Chair
Wood, metal and cowhide
57 x 7 1x 66 cm
Purchase, 2005 - AM 2005-1-17

Joe Colombo

| 1930, Milan (Italy)
| 1971, Milan (Italy)

• • • • • • • • • • • • • • • • • • •

Joe Colombo had already designed an armchair for the Zancope apartment in Milan when he opened his own architectural and interior design practice in that city in 1962.
The following year, in addition to his famous *Elda* chair, he designed *La Sella*, in which he put his researches into bent wood to the test: the chair marks the culmination of his experiments and the beginning of his collaboration with Comfort, this chair being the first prototype he developed with that manufacturer. Its seat, a single element of bent wood, stands on a base formed of two pieces of wood bent into C-shapes. Covered in cowhide, the seat contrasts with the two elements of the base, fixed to a leaf of metal that acts as a sprung support. The resulting flexibility responds to the movements of the user, in accordance with Colombo's conception of space, in which the furniture-environment should never exclude the dynamic aspect of the body: for him, "Man moves in space and lives in time." But *La Sella* was not easy to manufacture, notably on account of the torsion required and the difficulties of assembly. Given the high costs of production, it was only ever made to order, in limited numbers. But it would lead to the design of another metal product by Comfort, the *Supercomfort*, also called *Lem•* **MTMR**

Roger Tallon

| 1929, Paris (France)

· · · · · · · · · · · · · · · · · ·

In 1963, the television was still a very recent arrival, but Roger Tallon was already reinventing it. The task being to develop a portable model, he wanted something good to look at from every side, while until then a TV had been a rectangular box housing a tube with a bulky cowling at the back. At the front, Tallon extended the protective screen through the control panel. Formal beauty is combined with functionality, as in the designs Braun's Dieter Rams was producing at the same time. Visiting Tallon, his friend and neighbour, the sculptor César saw the prototype and thought it looked like a head without a neck, so the designer added one in the form of a little pedestal. The Fnac store decided to sell this little electronic sculpture at a low margin, which helped in its success, and it became one of the icons of the 1960s. In a France where everyone was talking about "industrial aesthetics," Roger Tallon was a pioneer of American-style design, integrated from the very moment of the product's conception. A "functionalist without ferocity," as he described himself, he would go on to design the Mexico City metro in 1967, and then spend almost thirty years as head of global design for the SNCF, the French railways. Amongst hundreds of projects, his responsibilities extended from the Corail intercity carriages and the TGV Duplex two-level high speed train to the logo and the platform signage • **XJ**

⬆ **1963**

Portavia P 111 Television

Manufacturer: Téléavia (France)
ABS and cellulose acetate butyrate
39 x 52 x 30 cm
19 cm (⌀, base)
Gift of M. Pierre Perrigault (Paris, France), 1992
AM 1993-1-407

Olivier Mourgue

1939, Paris (France)

· · · · · · · · · · · · · · · · · ·

As he was designing the *Djinn* series (chair, armchair, chaise longue, two-seater sofa, ottoman, coffee table and more), Olivier Mourgue was listening to the Beatles' *Yellow Submarine*. In 1968, Stanley Kubrick was planning for his futuristic film, *2001, A Space Odyssey*. He had seen the *Djinn* furniture, manufactured by Airborne, in a story about the designer's entirely white Paris apartment in the English magazine *Queen*. He hoped for a collaboration, and invited Mourgue and his wife to meet him at the studio where he was shooting in London. Named for the benevolent "genie" of Muslim belief, the *Djinn* designs illustrate Olivier Mourgue's interest in lightness, playfulness and modularity. In each of his projects (*Joker* in 1959, *Whist* in 1964-1965, *Montréal* in 1966 and again *Bouloum* in 1968), he developed a family of objects in which he emphasized the interplay between them. Mobility, the key to endless combinations, was for him an essential feature: a *Djinn* chair weighs 10 kilos. His projects testify to a generous quest for gaiety, in form as well as colour. The pieces of the *Djinn* series have removable covers of wool jersey, Mourgue selecting the shades from the range developed for Airborne by Bernard Joliet. For *2001, A Space Odyssey*, he offered Kubrick two reds – a vermilion and a Tyrian rose: "Kubrick liked red in a white interior." Also in the collection of MoMA, New York, the *Djinn* chaise longue won the First International Design Award in the United States • **CP**

1964-1965

Two-Seater Sofa
from the "Djinn" series
Manufacturer: Airborne
(France, 1964-1997)
Steel, rubber, polyurethane
foam and wool jersey
66 x 127 x 76 cm
Accession, 1993 - AM 1993-1-827

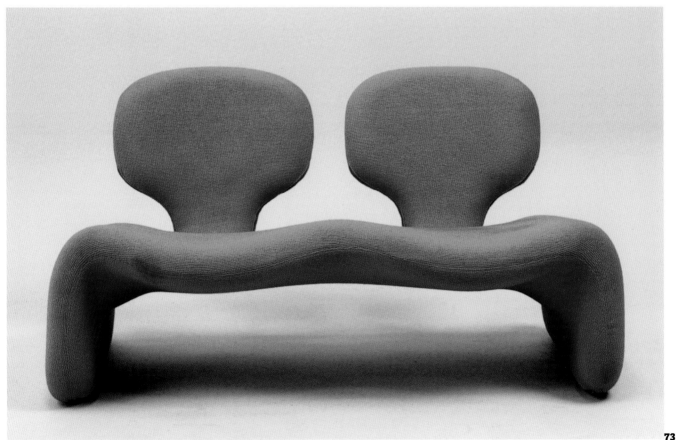

⟵ **1965**

Grillo Telephone
Manufactured for Italtel (Italy)
by Auso-Siemens (Italy)
ABS
18 x 22 x 8 cm
Purchase, 1995 - AM 1995-1-7

Richard Sapper, Marco Zanuso

Richard Sapper

| 1932, Munich (Germany)

Marco Zanuso

| 1916, Milan (Italy)
| 2001, Milan (Italy)

· · · · · · · · · · · · · · · · · · · ·

The designs of the Italian-German partnership of Zanuso and Sapper are characterised by the ambition to master technology so as to be able to integrate it seamlessly with user needs and the context of use. Employing, for the first time, a printed circuit and miniaturised electronic components, the *Grillo* telephone represents a culminating synthesis of their researches. In this respect, the *Grillo* may be said to have paved the way for today's smaller telephones and to have influenced contemporary mobile phones. Closed, the moulded ABS plastic shell fits in the palm of the hand, giving away little of its function. Open, it offers all the necessary elements: a microphone, a speaker, and a scaled-down dial with little dead space between the holes. Designed for the Italian national telephone system Italtel, the phone was manufactured by Auso-Siemens. Produced for only a short time, by reason of the cost of its innovations, it marked however a decisive turning point in telephony and communications design. It owed its name [*grillo* being Italian for cricket] not to its shape but to the chirp of its "ringer," incorporated in the wall-plug. The phone won the Compasso d'Oro in 1967 • **MTMR**

Pierre Paulin

1927, Paris (France)
2009, Montpellier (France)

• • • • • • • • • • • • • • • • • •

Joie de vivre, inventiveness and purity of line: the whole spirit of the 1960s. This sculptural chair with its ribbon form incorporates two important technical innovations: the foam rubber wrapped around the steel frame on its wooden base, and the cover of stretch jersey. Some years earlier, Pierre Paulin had had the idea of using a bathing-costume fabric for upholstery, and in the mid-1960s he met the American textile designer Jack Lenor Larsen and began a fruitful collaboration with him. The *Ribbon Chair* was thus covered in a variety of coloured patterns, whose swirling lines coincide with the advent of psychedelia. Its supple form and

restrained eroticism recall Art Nouveau, then being enthusiastically rediscovered after decades of neglect. But this chair is above all the fruit of Paulin's meeting with Harry Wagemans, head of the Dutch manufacturers Artifort. After a period with Thonet, Pierre Paulin – strongly inspired by the simplicity of Nordic design and despairing of the chance to fully express his talents in France – was recruited in 1959 by the Maastricht firm, whose furniture he revolutionised without ever losing sight of the essentials: a chair had to be comfortable. Like other timeless pieces by Paulin (*Mushroom*, 1960 and *Tongue*, 1967), the *Ribbon Chair* is again being produced today by its original manufacturer • **XJ**

⊘ **1966**

**Ribbon Chair
(model 582)**
Manufacturer: Artifort (Netherlands)
Maker, fabric: Jack Lenor Larsen (United Stades)
Steel, latex foam, polyamide jersey and wood
70 x 105 x 80 cm
Gift of Strafor (Strasbourg, France), 1996 - AM 1996-1-3

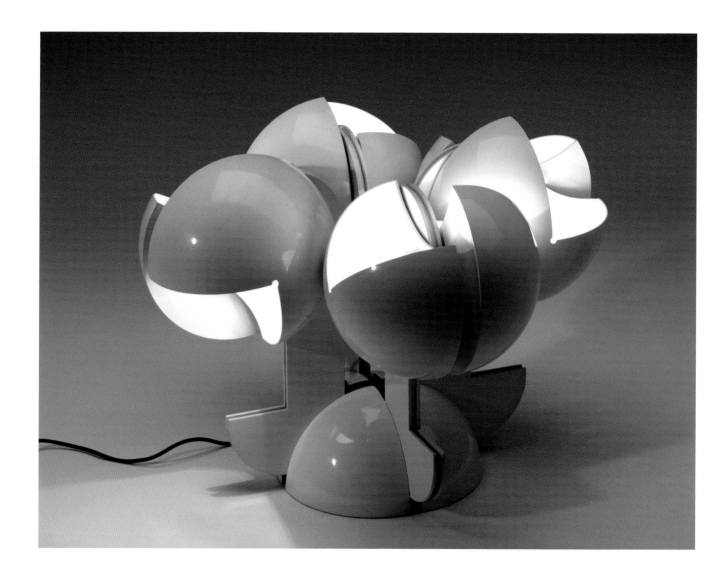

Gae Aulenti

| 1927, Palazzolo dello Stella (Italy)

• • • • • • • • • • • • • • • • • • •

Designer, architect, stage designer and teacher, Gae Aulenti was a member of the editorial committee of *Casabella Continuità*, and then of the magazine *Lotus International*. Creator of interiors for Olivetti, Knoll and Fiat in the 1960s and 1970s, but also of designs for theatre and opera, it was she who transformed the Gare d'Orsay railway station in Paris into a national art museum. Critical of Modernism's rejection of historic styles and references, she draws inspiration in her design from sources of different kinds and registers. Her *Sgarsul* rocking chair (1962), for example, makes reference to Thonet bentwood furniture, while the smooth surfaces and the lines of her celebrated *Pipistrello* lamp (1965) recall the Vienna Secession. In *Ruspa*

["bulldozer"], Aulenti offers a lamp that suggests an early-20th-century avant-garde sculpture as much as it does a robot or a hairdryer. Its most remarkable feature is the spherical shade divided into two reflectors, each holding a bulb. The *Ruspa* lamp might make one think of Vico Magistretti's best-selling *Eclipse* light, even if the latter is less complex, more archetypal and smaller in scale. The moveable parts of Aulenti's lamp allow the direction and intensity of light to be adjusted. When four are set together, the *Ruspa* lamp presents a more abstract and more sculptural aspect • **PT**

⚘ **1967**

Ruspa Lamp
Manufacturer: Martinelli Luce (Italy)
Aluminium
58 cm (h) x 30 cm (ø)
Gift of the artist, 2009
AM 2009-1-112

Haus-Rucker-Co

Laurids Ortner
| 1941, Linz (Austria)

Klaus Pinter
| 1940, Schärding am Inn (Austria)

Günter Zamp Kelp
| 1941, Bistriţa (Romania)

Haus-Rucker-Co (1967-1992) was joined in 1971 by :

Manfred Ortner
| 1943, Linz (Austria)

• • • • • • • • • • • • • • •

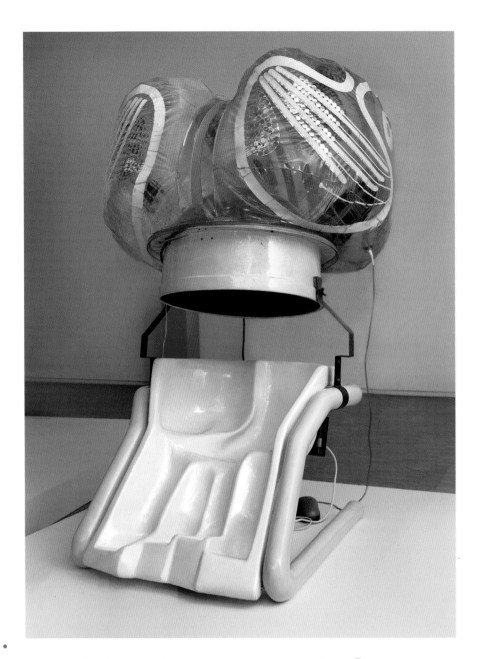

Mindexpander 1 was designed in 1967 for a competition staged by a German firm on the theme of living space in the year 2000. The two-seater chair is surmounted by what might be a giant hairdryer with a Plexiglas dome, itself surrounded by a PVC balloon recalling the lobes of the brain, the whole providing aural and visual stimuli. Seen from inside, the red and blue motifs overlapping at different levels were to create a state resembling hypnosis. A portable version, the *Flyhead*, was developed in 1968. In the age of space exploration and the first man on the moon, *Mindexpander 1* was intended to expand consciousness and explore inner space. It is to some degree a mechanical equivalent of the hallucinogenic drugs with which the artistic avant-garde were then experimenting. It can also be seen as the distant ancestor of the virtual reality headset and other high-tech prostheses. Founded in 1967, Haus-Rucker-Co was a Viennese collective of artists and architects who created cognitive pieces such as an inflatable *Love Divan* and a *Giant Billiards* for 100 people. Between design, architecture and contemporary art, the group's much publicised installations were occasions for performances in which the public participated. The group's prolific and influential work was associated with a critique of industrial society. It dissolved in 1992 • **XJ**

⊕ **1967**

Mindexpander 1
PVC and fibreglass-reinforced polyester
210 x 140 x 160 cm
Purchase, 2000 - AM 2000-2-149

⬆ 1967

Culbuto Chair

Manufacturer: Knoll Associates
(United States)
Fibreglass-reinforced polyester
and leather
114 x 80 x 90 cm
Gift of the Société des Amis du
Musée National d'Art Moderne
(Paris, France), 1999 - AM 1998-1-11

Marc Held

| 1932, Paris (France)

• •

Following a visit in 1965 to the Fritz
Hansen factory, where engineers were
working on joints that would allow
chairs by Danish designer Arne
Jacobsen to both turn and tilt, Marc
Held came up with the idea of doing
away with conventional legs or bases
altogether by giving the chair a

ballasted convex bottom. In 1967,
he designed such a double-shelled
armchair in fibreglass-reinforced
polyester resin. The upper shell,
upholstered in foam rubber and jersey,
fits into the lower. The occupant can
shift about as desired and avoid or
relieve any stiffness due to immobility.
Shown at the designer's own Paris shop,
the first prototype attracted the
attention of Florence Knoll and Yves
Vidal, head of Knoll International
France, who asked him to pursue work
on the idea. The next three years saw
a dialogue established between the
American firm and the French designer,
a collaboration that led to the *Culbuto*
series, comprising an ottoman and two
armchairs – one with a high back, the
other with a low back – which went
into production in 1970. Apart from
the textile designer Jacqueline Iribe,
Marc Held is the only French designer
whose work has been taken up by Knoll
International • **MD**

• •

Ugo La Pietra

| 1938, Bussi sul Tirino (Italy)

• • • • • • • • • • • • • • • • • •

Created in 1967, the *Globo Tissurato*
[Textured Globe] lamp is an imaginative
and critical piece typical of the work
of artist, architect and designer Ugo
La Pietra, whose provocative approach
aims to disrupt customary habits. Like
his *Immersions*, conceived around
the same time – spheres or helmets
incorporating means of powerful
audio-visual stimulation – this is an
instrument of sensual experiment.
In making these pieces, Ugo La Pietra
experimented in his studio with
methacrylate, a transparent synthetic
material in which he created
elementary geometrical, modular forms.
Three identical hemispheres
surrounded by a transparent cylinder

make up the structure of the lamp. One
at the bottom, resting on the base,
contains the electric bulb, the light
being adjustable with a dimmer. The
two others form a single sphere,
supported at the circumference by the
top of the cylinder, so being suspended
a little above the light source that finds
itself reflected in them. All three are
textured by a regular grid of holes
across the surface that accentuates the
thrum of the light and the sense of the
object's dissolution into space. A
weightless bubble, the lamp loses its
identity. A source of diffuse light, it is
at the same time transfigured,
suggesting other images than its own in
the ludic space of an object
emancipated of its primary function
and delivered up to the
imagination • **AMZ**

➔ 1967

Globo Tissurato
Lamp

Manufacturer: Kriliko Design
(Italy)
Distributor: Promet S.R.L. (Italy)
Methacrylate
72 cm (h) x 40.5 cm (ø)
Purchase, 2009 - AM 2009-1-56

Andrea Branzi

| 1939, Florence (Italy)

Gilberto Corretti

| 1941, Florence (Italy)

Paolo Deganello

| 1940, Este (Italy)

Massimo Morozzi

| 1941, Florence (Italy)

Established in 1966, Archizoom Associati was joined in 1968 by:

Dario Bartolini

| 1943, Trieste (Italy)

Lucia Bartolini

| 1944, Florence (Italy)

· · · · · · · · · · · · · · · ·

⬇ 1968

Safari Sofa

Manufacturer: Poltronova (Italy)
Fibreglass-reinforced polyester,
polyurethane foam and
synthetic fabric
64 x 254 x 214 cm
Gift of Strafor (Strasbourg,
France), 1999 - AM 1999-1-1

The *Safari* sofa is typical of the provocative anti-design creations of Archizoom. This Italian avant-gardist group, established in Florence in 1966 by Andrea Branzi, Gilberto Corretti, Paolo Deganello and Massimo Morozzi, was part of the current that emerged in the 1970s to criticize the Modern Movement, putting its dogmas and its icons into question. In design, as in architecture, the group stood for subversion, radicalism and utopia. Understood as a modular and flexible space for living, and conceived in the spirit of Pop Art, the *Safari* sofa thus has a deliberately kitsch side. Far from functionalist, its four elements of fibreglass-reinforced polyester resin – two square and two rectangular – together form a large white block. Upholstered in polyurethane foam, the single and double seats are as it were scooped out of this, their form mischievously delineating a flower, though covered ironically enough in a synthetic, leopard-skin print. Through both form and colour, the seating succeeds in lightening the massive geometry of the structure. The sofa was manufactured in Italy by Poltronova. Artisanal in its production, the company made the sofas individually as orders were received ● **MTMR**

1968

Déclive

Aluminium, lacquered steel,
polyether foam and wool fabric
100 x 320 x 140 cm
Purchase, 2003 - AM 2003-1-309

Pierre Paulin

| 1927, Paris (France)
| 2009, Montpellier (France)

• • • • • • • • • • • • • • • •

The idea of giant modular seating for
multiple occupants was typical of the
thinking of the 1960s, a time of utopias
and of revolutionary changes in how
people lived. The modern man and
woman were exploring and
rediscovering their bodies. They let
themselves go, they sought to "live close
to the ground…" In 1966, Roger Tallon
had thus come up with his *Lit
métamorphique trapézoïdal*, which
remained a prototype. That same year,
Bernard Gauvin created *Asmara*, a vast,
undulant sofa for Roset. Pierre Paulin's

Déclive was shown at the Salon du
Meuble of 1968 by French manufacturer
Mobilier International. A low platform,
a "deformable surface," you could sit on
it as on a sofa, or lie down, or face each
other… Anything was possible! The
Déclive flexes on two backbones of
aluminium (there is also a version using
plastic), but it proved to be too fragile
for mass production, and only three
examples are known to exist. In the
same spirit, Paulin conceived in 1980 a
rug-cum-seating for American
manufacturer Herman Miller. In
between, and in a different register, he
produced in 1971 another masterpiece:
the interior design of the private
apartments at the Élysée Palace,
commissioned by President Pompidou
and his wife • xj

Ettore Sottsass

1917, Innsbruck (Austria)
2007, Milan (Italy)

• • • • • • • • • • • • • • • • • • •

Altare (Molto Privato) was shown at the exhibition "Landscape for a New Planet" (Stockholm, 1969). Geometrical and symmetrical in composition this piece in a delicate yellow is identified as an altar, unrelated to any Modernist typology but associated with domestic worship. In a preparatory drawing, Sottsass indicates that *Altare (Molto Privato)* could be used for the storage of precious personal mementos. On either side of this altar with its subtle play of levels, the user seeking to engage in recollection can meditate on a seat composed of horizontal, vertical

and oblique planes. The rigor of the design is softened by the presence of four *Asteroid* lamps, a model created by Sottsass in 1968, characterised by its U-shaped neon tube. Rising from bases of painted metal, the four lights – two red and two pink – are arranged in inverse symmetry. They confer on the piece an effect of surprise, an aura even. "The idea," wrote Sottsass, "was to expand the concept of function to embrace both conscious and unconscious, something the Bauhaus and all that generation never thought to do" • **PT**

⬆ **1968**

Altare (Molto Privato)
One-off piece
Print laminate, plywood, rubber and lamps
135 x 320 x 135 cm
Purchase, 2003 - AM 2002-1-61

➜ **1968**

Gherpe Lamp
Prototype
Perspex and metal
64 x 45 x 29 cm
Purchase, 2001 - AM 2001-1-159

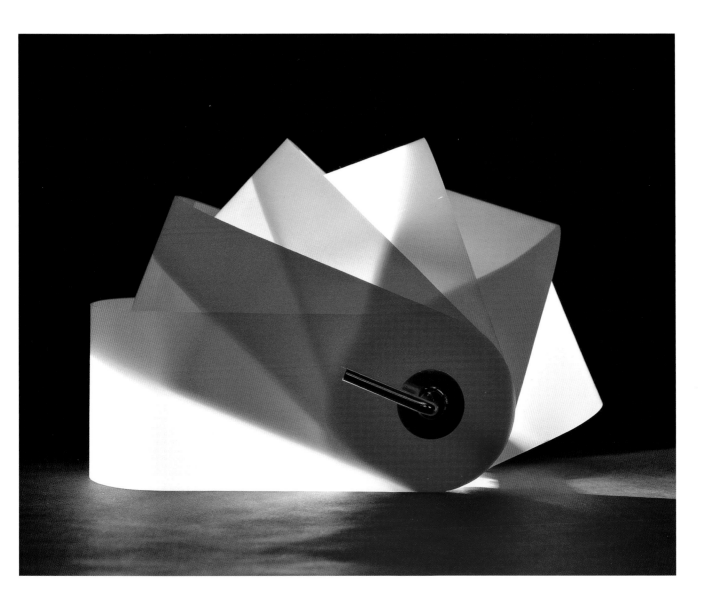

Superstudio

Adolfo Natalini

| 1941, Pistoia (Italy)

Cristiano Toraldo di Francia

| 1941, Florence (Italy)

Superstudio, established in 1966, was later joined by:

Roberto Magris

| 1935, Florence (Italy)

Gian Piero Frassinelli

| 1939, Porto San Giorgio (Italy)

Alessandro Magris

| 1941, Florence (Italy)

Alessandro Poli

| 1941, Florence (Italy)

Established in Florence in 1966, Superstudio was, like Archizoom Associati, one of the founding groups of radical Italian architecture. Its members – Adolfo Natalini and Cristiano Toraldo di Francia, later joined by Roberto Magris (from 1967 to 1986), Gian Piero Frassinelli (from 1968 to 1986), Alessandro Magris (from 1970 to 1986) and Alessandro Poli (from 1970 to 1972) and – stood opposed to modern functionalism, developing a critique of it in architecture, design and urbanism. To rationalistic planning, Superstudio preferred improvisation and a certain hedonism, a hedonism evident in the sensuality of the *Gherpe* lamp, intended for a younger market. Without any base, it is distinguished by its materials, chrome-plated steel and acrylic, the latter being pink, a favourite colour of the 1960s and 1970s excluded from the design of the preceding decades. *Gherpe* offers a range of configurations, its fluorescent bands opening or closing to vary the intensity of light. The influence of Pop Art is visible in this lamp that is both "witty" and "sexy," in the words of Richard Hamilton's famous definition, which also might also suggest some futuristic helmet. Like the *Bazaar* seating environment of 1969-1970, the *Gherpe* lamp preceded a period of intense theoretical research, during which Superstudio critically developed "neutral designs, then, finally, negative utopias, premonitory images of the horrors that architecture was holding in store for us, with its scientific methods for the perpetuation of existing models • **PT**

1969

Pilastro Totem
One-off piece
Ceramic
215 cm (h) x 200 cm (ø)
Purchase, 2003 - AM 2002-1-62

Ettore Sottsass

1917, Innsbruck (Austria)
2007, Milan (Italy)

· · · · · · · · · · · · · · · · · ·

A collaborator rather than a lone pioneer in the world of radical Italian design, Ettore Sottsass was a consultant to Olivetti and Poltronova, a founder of the Global Tools counter-school of architecture and design, a member of Studio Alchimia and joint founder of the Memphis Group. Known too for his drawings, photographs, installations and conceptual projects, he prioritized meaning over form, insisting that the object should not be hegemonized by reason. Much of his work testifies to a great diversity of inspiration, drawing on philosophy and anthropology but also on Indian culture, Beat culture and Pop Art. Consisting of five identical columns arranged around a shorter but wider central column, the *Pilastro Totem* seems to escape any function but the symbolic. This large-scale ceramic is the fruit of a project for a "Pillar to be installed on the frontier of the country of non-violence," conceived for the "Landscape for a New Planet" exhibition (Stockholm, 1969). Each column consists of a stack of discs, suggesting the Minimalist principle of seriality, though the use that Sottsass makes of repetition is much more expressive. The dark blue colour and the light glistening on the surface emphasize the sensuality of a piece simultaneously primitive, sculptural and luxurious in finish • **PT**

Mario Bellini

1935, Milan (Italy)

· · · · · · · · · · · · · · · · · ·

Mario Bellini is best known for his work as an industrial designer, before he began in the 1980s to focus more on architectural projects. Postmodern in inspiration, his buildings (among them the Villa Erba conference centre on the shores of Lake Como, the Tokyo Design Center, the Portello complex at the Milan Fair, Natuzzi's American headquarters), conceived as imaginative glazed structures, are fragments inserted into the city understood as urban fabric. A teacher too, Bellini was also editor of the magazine *Domus* from 1986 to 1991. In the field of design, he distinguished himself by his inventive use of materials and by his interest in sensual experience rather than in strictly functionalist solutions. During the 1960s and 1970s, he designed a stereo set reflecting the anti-establishment thinking of the time, as well as furniture, lighting, calculators, a computer terminal, and even a car punningly known as the *Kar-a-Sutra* (around 1971). The *Teneride* chair, which got no further than the prototype stage (perhaps because of its being disagreeable to the touch) was the result of researches on the production of monobloc seating in polyurethane. Its eloquent form made more expressive yet by the use of the colour red, balanced on a single central spot on its circular base, the *Teneride* chair unfurls itself in accordion-like folds, the outside being echoed within • **PT**

➔ 1970

Teneride Chair
Prototype
Manufacturer: Cassina (Italy)
Polyurethane foam and wood
95 x 67 x 63 cm
52 cm (ø, base)
Gift of Cassina (Meda, Italy), 1992
AM 1992-1-355

Side 1 and Side 2

Manufacturers: Fujiko (Japan),
Cappellini (Italy, after 1986)
Ash wood and steel
Gift of Cappellini (Arosio, Italy),
1996
Side 1 (right): AM 1996-1-11
Side 2 (left): AM 1996-1-12

Shiro Kuramata

1934, Tokyo (Japan)
1991, Tokyo (Japan)

Shiro Kuramata began by working for big Japanese companies before setting up his own firm in 1965. While his early designs evidence a distinctive interest in wood, he quickly came to employ a range of materials, among them synthetic resins, glass and steel mesh, put to post-Minimal, decorative use. During the 1980s, Shiro Kuramata collaborated with the Italian Memphis Group and then designed interiors, for Issey Miyake's shops, for instance. Taking, but also playing with, the form of the chiffonier – a tall chest of drawers – *Side 1* and *Side 2* are the height of a human figure. Apparently complementary, their undulating lines can only be married anti-functionally, the side of *Side 1* fitting only the front of *Side 2*, whose drawers it would prevent from opening. Produced by Fujiko in 1970, and then re-issued by Cappellini in 1986, they stand on castors, as did the *Pyramid Furniture* chest of drawers (1968), just a little taller. This mobility allows the user to remodel the surrounding space. They thus simultaneously instance both the Modernist idea of design as the conception of functional equipment and a notion of the decorative arts, as evidenced by their forms and by the contrast of black and white they offer • **PT**

Verner Panton

1926, Brahesborg-Gamtofte (Denmark)
1998, Copenhagen (Denmark)

• • • • • • • • • • • • • • • • •

A major figure in 1960s and 1970s design, Verner Panton began by training as an architect at the Royal Danish Academy in Copenhagen, under renowned architect and designer Arne Jacobsen. In 1955, he opened his own design office in the same city, where he stayed until 1962. After a brief spell working in Paris, in 1963 he settled in Switzerland. A many-sided designer, he worked simultaneously on interior design, furniture, textiles and colour – his favourite field.

Conceived in 1970-1971 for the living room of his home in Basel, the *Living Sculpture* embodies the period's new way of inhabiting domestic space – collectively and close to the ground. Panton created a dwelling place, an embracing structure, a monumental sculpture of impressive size (220 x 510 x 430 cm) whose looping meanders are enlivened by bright, saturated colours and psychedelic motifs. In a dialogue of solids and voids that plays too on effects of scale, Panton creates depths and perspectives that undermine any unambiguous reading of the volume. A playful one-of-a-kind, this *Living Sculpture*, with its innovative idea of space, is intended as an occasion of new sensual experience, both visual and auditory – the polyurethane foam covered in a wool weave being a sound-absorber. The piece was shown at the Cologne Furniture Show in 1972 • **CP**

⊌ 1970-1971

Living Sculpture
One-off piece
Makers: Kill & Metzeler
(Germany), Mira-X (Switzerland)
Wool weave, polyether foam,
plywood and polystyrene
220 x 510 x 430 cm
Gift of Strafor (Strasbourg,
France), 1992 - AM 1992-1-409

design français

centre de création
industrielle

design architectural,
industriel, intérieur,
graphique.

pavillon de marsan
palais du louvre
107 rue de rivoli, paris
22 oct. – 20 déc. 71

jean widmer

→ **1971**

**"Design français"
Poster**

Silkscreen print
65 x 50 cm
Accession, 1992 - AM 1993-1-317 (1)

Jean Widmer

▮ 1929, Frauenfeld (Switzerland)

• • • • • • • • • • • • • • • • • •

When the Centre de Création Industrielle, then housed at the Musée des Arts Décoratifs, turned to him in 1969 for a series of posters for their design exhibitions, Jean Widmer had just left his job as artistic director of the magazine *Jardin des modes* to start his own firm. Informed by the basic principles of design, drawing on elementary figures and archetypal forms, he developed a kind of modular grid that allowed him to design his posters with the same basic framework and a range of geometrical figures (squares, triangles, circles) variously assembled. He thus divided the surface of each poster into twelve squares, the upper quarter being reserved for the text, the rest for the image. Far from being intended to represent an object, this assemblage of simplified forms in bright, contrasting colours strove to give symbolic expression, through its extreme stylization, to the theme of the exhibition concerned.

In this poster for the exhibition "Design français," in the colours of the French flag, the idea of "architectural, industrial, interior and graphic design," is evoked through forms reduced to their essence. The twenty-one posters designed by Jean Widmer between 1969 and 1975 all share this same graphic coherence, which identifies the Centre de Création Industrielle even before any message has been communicated • **MD**

Oscar Niemeyer

I 1907, Rio de Janeiro (Brazil)

· · · · · · · · · · · · · · · · · ·

In 1972, Oscar Niemeyer designed an armchair with footstool, the first furniture of an architect especially distrustful of mass production. Fleeing the Brazilian military dictatorship, in 1967 he settled in France, where he opened a Paris office that he would keep on when he returned home in 1979. There he worked on projects that reflected his own political commitments: the headquarters of the French Communist Party and the offices of its newspaper *L'Humanité*, the Bourse du Travail in Bobigny and the very first of the Maisons de la Culture (cultural centres) to be established by André Malraux, at Le Havre.

The fruit of a collaboration between Niemeyer and his daughter Anna-Maria and the French architects and interior designers Claude Bond and François Foucher, this chair would go into the entrance hall of the *L'Humanité* building, built in 1989. It consists of a broad, curved, springy blade, first made of moulded wood, later of stainless steel. Neither rigid nor static, this blade supports both seat and backrest, and gives the form of the chair its lightness. The separate seat and back are upholstered in expanded polyurethane and covered in leather. The chair was first manufactured by Mobilier International, which offered it in high and low models. From 1978, it would be offered in two versions – one in bent wood – by the Japanese Tendo Mokko, manufacturers of furniture in moulded ply, who set up a production unit in Brazil: Tendo Brasileira • **AMZ**

⊘ **1972**

Chair
Wood, leather, cotton felt
and polyester foam
73 x 73 x 106 cm
Gift of *L'Humanité* (France), 2009
AM 2009-1-22

Golgotha Chair
Prototype
"Golgotha" collection
Manufacturer: Bracciodiferro
(Italy)
Dacron-filled and resin-soaked
fibreglass cloth
75 x 45 x 58 cm
Gift of Cassina (Meda, Italy), 1992
AM 1992-1-358

Gaetano Pesce

▎ 1939, La Spezia (Italy)

• • • • • • • • • • • • • • • • •

Gaetano Pesce challenges and provokes, making one laugh and making one think. "The designer wants to make perfect objects, but we find that neither objects nor ourselves are perfect, so that kind of object is incapable of communicating anything at all. It communicates only… that it is artificial," he has said. In the early 1970s, this architect-artist-designer thus started to design mass-produced unique objects. For the *Golgotha* chair (whose name evokes the Passion and the seamless robe of Christ) a length of fibreglass cloth was soaked by hand in resin, and then draped over strings, like linen drying. Hardened, the folds vary from one chair to another. An opponent of functionalism and an enemy of the industrial production he denounces as totalitarian, Gaetano Pesce is nonetheless an enthusiastic user of contemporary materials, which he experiments with in every possible way. While the *Golgotha* chair is made of resin, his famous *Up5* chair, for example, is made of polyurethane foam: delivered flat, it takes up its shape on contact with air, the buyer participating in the act of its creation. Its generous curves thus suggest a female body, but one that is attached to a pouffe as to a ball-and-chain, to show that a woman is "always. a prisoner of herself against her will." This feminist discourse is typical of this Italian designer, who moved to New York in 1980, where he is still active today ● **XJ**

Michel Cadestin

1942, Épernay (France)

In 1974, Michel Cadestin entered the international competition for the design of office furniture for the Centre Pompidou, which would open in 1977. He had earlier worked in partnership with designer Michel Ragot, with whom, until 1970, he had developed new forms of living space using plastic inflatables and foam rubber of varying densities: an example is the famous *Alcove 2000* – a prototype bedroom with floor and wall in tubes of polyurethane foam. When the competition was announced, he had been since 1973 head of design at interior design house Teda. To meet the requirements, he decided to team up with small manufacturers to create specifically for the Centre a range of fire-resistant office furniture (tables and chairs) in metal and leather. He thus turned to the Laurent company, with whom he developed the *Traîneau Chair*, and its variant, the *Dactylo Chair* on castors, put on the market by Teda in 1976.

The structure of the *Traîneau Chair* is of galvanised steel rod welded into a grille, with seat and back pads in Argentine leather. The *Dactylo Chair* is upholstered in foam. Cadestin would complete the range with the *Président* armchair and stool, made by Ere Form, and a desk, made in collaboration with Aselbur and Polyrey. He won the competition with this furniture, which would remain in use at the Centre Pompidou until 1997 • **MD**

⇩ 1976

Traîneau Chair
Made for Éditions Teda (France)
by Laurent (France)
Steel and leather
73 x 59 x 55 cm
Accession, 2002
AM 2002-1-33

Kandissi Sofa
Manufacturer: Studio Alchimia (Italy)
Wood, leather and tapestry
99 x 205 x 87 cm
25 x 158 x 77 cm (base)
Gift of Strafor (Strasbourg,
France), 1997 - AM 1997-1-94

Alessandro Mendini

❙ 1931, Milan (Italy)
● ● ● ● ● ● ● ● ● ● ● ● ● ● ● ●

Involved in the establishment of the Global Tools design education and research group, Alessandro Mendini was also one of the founders of Studio Alchimia and editor of the magazines *Casabella*, *Modo* and then *Domus*. In 1979, he showed his *Poltrona di Proust* chair and the *Kandissi* sofa at the "Bau. Haus" exhibition in Milan. The first was the result of a "redesign" exercise in which a Louis XV armchair in buttoned leather was painted over in a pointillist design inspired by the work of Paul Signac. The chair finds itself re-energized by the addition of this pictorial element that has nothing to do with its form or function. This was for Mendini a way of abolishing the difference between function and painted decor and a superimposition of heterogeneous cultural references. The *Kandissi* sofa is an asymmetrical construction based to some extent on a principle of fragmentation foreign to the modernist quest for unity. Decorated with pennants and geometric motifs, it is inspired by the structural role of areas of flat colour in Kandinsky's painting. Aggressive yet appealing, with its angular planes and irregular outlines, the sofa has an upholstered seat and back covered in a moiré-patterned fabric. Highly expressive, it presents a deliberate discord of tone that puts into question generally accepted ideas of good and bad taste, rejecting the restrictive conventions of the furniture industry ● **PT**

"Paris-Paris 1937-1957" Poster
Silkscreen
70 x 50 cm
Government purchase, 1991
Attribution to Centre Pompidou,
Musée National d'Art Moderne-
Centre de Création Industrielle,
2008 - AM 2009-1-208

Roman Cieslewicz

1930, Lvov (Poland, today Ukraine)
1996, Malakoff (France)

Trained at the Academy of Fine Arts in Krakow, where his education was much influenced by the avant-gardist legacy of Polish Constructivism, Roman Cieslewicz began by designing posters for political, cultural and social purposes. Arriving in Paris in the early 1960s, he was rapidly recognized as a politically engaged, if not subversive, graphic designer, and he worked there for the theatre and the cinema, but also for the press, publishing and advertising. He became artistic director of *Elle*, then of *Opus international*, of the Mafia agency and co-author, with Christian Bourgois, of the ephemeral "panic news review" *Kamikaze*. Alongside his commissioned work, he developed his thinking on the image in photomontages sometimes inspired by Pop Art and in experimental works in which news photographs were combined with fragments of classical painting. His work for the Centre Pompidou between 1978 and 1983 is characterised by compositions based on disequilibrium in which the typography is treated as a "visual mass." With his poster for the "Paris-Paris" exhibition he returns, in reversing it, to the diagonal composition used two years earlier for the "Paris-Moscow" poster. On a yellow ground, a mirrored but truncated Eiffel Tower serves as the principal axis, echoing too the inversion of the lettering. In 1993, three years before the his death, the Centre Pompidou devoted a significant exhibition to the designer's work • **PT**

→ **1981**

Barbare Chair

Manufacturer: Galerie Néotù
(France)
Iron and horsehide
118 x 57 x 50 cm
Purchase, 1992 - AM 1992-1-249

Garouste & Bonetti

Élisabeth Garouste

| 1949, Paris (France)

Mattia Bonetti

| 1952, Lugano (Switzerland)

The partnership ended in 2001

Élisabeth Garouste and Mattia Bonetti gained attention for their critical approach to the fundamental criteria of modernism (functionalism, technical innovation, mass production, the rejection of ornament) with their first exhibition, at the Galerie Jansen (Paris, 1981). The *Barbare* chair is emblematic of their work at that time; its name saw its creators dubbed "the New Barbarians" by the press. Produced in a run of 100, it combines a deliberate primitivism and a certain return to the natural with a high quality finish. The frame of greenish patinated wrought iron is surmounted by symbolic decorations suggestive of horns, and laced onto it with pale brown leather thongs is a horsehide that serves as seat and backrest. Close to craft art, this markedly expressive piece has a narrative dimension. Described as "Neo-Baroque," the *Barbare* chair suggests a throne – as also will the very different *Prince Impérial* chair (1985) – in this case of African inspiration. The inclusion of eclectic cultural references in their furniture and in the pieces they designed for industry made Garouste and Bonetti original exponents of the French decorative tradition. The diverse contributions of these two designers, who ended their partnership in 2001 after more than 20 years of working together, is one of the most audacious reactions against the standardisation of industrial production • **PT**

Martin Szekely

1956, Paris (France)

Furniture was reinvented in the early 1980s. The gloss of the Pop years was brusquely rejected, the oil crisis encouraged the use of materials other than plastic, and computer-aided design took its first tentative steps: the *Pi* chaise longue gives expression to all these developments. Its convexity is not immediately welcoming, putting into question our notions of sitting or reclining. On seeing it, furniture dealer Pierre Staudenmeyer cried out: "C'est néo, néo, néo tout!", thereby finding the name under which his gallery would become famous: Néotù. Martin Szekely's chaise longue was the first piece he had manufactured. Shown at the Milan International Furniture Show of 1985, and elsewhere across the world, it became an icon of the time and the symbol of the revival of French design. As Staudenmeyer noted, with this chair, Martin Szekely – the son of a sculptor, trained at the École Boulle and the École Estienne – faced up to not only his paternal heritage but to that of Breuer and Le Corbusier, founding fathers of modernity. What is more, while the *Pi* chaise longue is inspired by the same desire for visual economy, its design is so radically simplified as to form a sign, a logo. Some years later, Martin Szekely decided to withdraw behind his objects, pursuing, alongside his interest in furniture, a discreet but highly productive career as an industrial designer, with creations as diverse as street furniture, a glass for Perrier and two-seater chairs for an MK2 cinema • **XJ**

1982-1983

Pi Chaise Longue
"Pi" collection
Manufacturer: Galerie Néotù (France)
Steel, aluminium and leather
84 x 64 x 140 cm
Purchase, 1992 - AM 1992-1-247

Tolomeo Table Lamp
Prototype
Manufacturer: Artemide (Italy)
Metal
60 x 80 x 20 cm
Gift of M. Ernesto Gismondi
(Milan, Italy), 2004
AM 2003-1-395

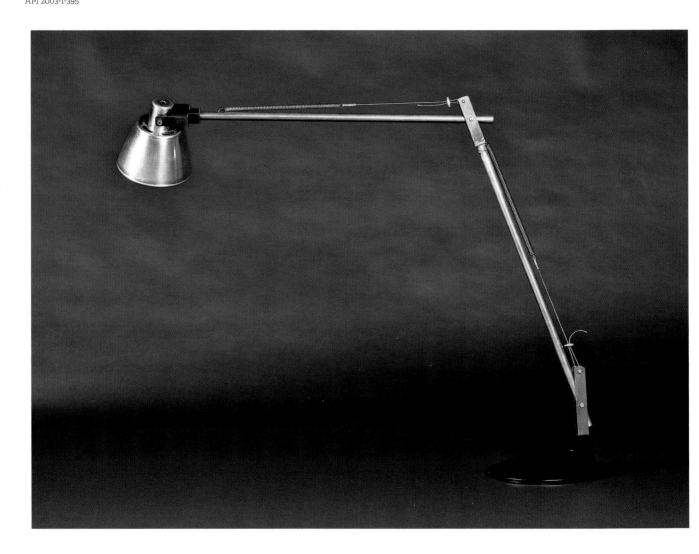

Michele De Lucchi

| 1951, Ferrare (Italy)

● ● ● ● ● ● ● ● ● ● ● ● ● ● ● ● ●

With the *Tolomeo* table lamp, conceived as "a technological object with a human feel," Michele De Lucchi concentrated all his attention on tension and movement, on articulation and adjustability. In its form, with its clean and elegant lines, the metal prototype in the collection of the Centre

Pompidou prefigures the lamp that De Lucchi would design with Giancarlo Fassina for Artemide in 1986, to win the Compasso d'Oro three years later, in 1989. It has a reflector of matt anodized aluminium, an articulated structure of the same metal, polished, and a spring mechanism hidden within the arms. It is today available in different forms – table lamp, floor lamp, wall or ceiling light – and its quarter-century of success shows no sign of coming to an end. The *Tolomeo* lamp afforded yet more evidence of Michele De Lucchi's capacity to emancipate

himself from style, to conceive a design in complete freedom. A creator who defies boundaries and disciplinary demarcations, he is an architect as well as a designer, working in both the public and private sectors, who exploits not only technology but also craft skills to explore and experiment in every field. Similarly, the *Tolomeo* lamp takes a deliberate distance from the whimsical imagination characteristic of the Memphis Group that the designer had founded two years earlier, in 1981, together with Ettore Sottsass and Andrea Branzi • **MTMR**

J. Armchair
"Lang" series
Manufacturer: Driade (Italy)
Cast aluminium, steel,
polyurethane foam and leather
86 x 60 x 66 cm
Gift of Driade (Fossadello
di Caorso, Italy), 1999
AM 1999-1-150

Philippe Starck

ǀ 1949, Paris (France)

• •

Not just an industrial designer, Philippe
Starck has been responsible for the
interiors of the Paris nightclubs La
Main Bleue et Les Bains-Douches, and
also of Café Costes and some of the
private apartments of the Élysée Palace
in the same city, hotels in New York,
and boats for Beneteau. As an architect,
he has notably designed the Nani Nani,
Asahi and Le Baron Vert buildings in
Japan, and was involved in the design
of the Gröninger Museum in the
Netherlands. Collaborating with many
design houses and manufacturers,
Starck has been involved in nearly
every area of modern material life,
oscillating between a Minimalism in
search of the archetypal and a more
expressive approach that sometimes
has recourse to historical citations
tinged with irony. His *J.* chair belongs
to the "Lang" series, commissioned by
the Mobilier National – the French state
furniture collection – when Jack Lang
was Minister of Culture. A shell of
tubular steel is upholstered in
polyurethane foam covered in black
leather. Of the three legs of cast
aluminium, only the back leg is visible.
The structure is thus hidden, in
contravention of modernist principle,
and Starck creates an opposition
between the front and back, an
opposition of which one could say, as
Starck did of his *Richard III* chair (1985):
"In front, [the solidity of] the
bourgeoisie, and when you turn around,
behind, the void" • **PT**

Racing Motorcycle
Yamaha prototype
Fibreglass-reinforced polyester
130 x 260 x 75 cm
Gift of Strafor (Strasbourg,
France), 1992 - AM 1992-1-413

Luigi Colani

(Lutz Colani, known as)

| 1928, Berlin (Germany)

• • • • • • • • • • • • • • • • • • • •

After studying aerodynamics in Paris, the German designer Luigi Colani caused a sensation in the 1950s with his futuristic designs for cars and motorcycles. Inspired by nature, in which he saw neither straight lines nor sharp edges, his whole thinking has been based on the optimal relationship between man and object: this underlies an ergonomic bio-design of fluid lines that has had a great influence on contemporary design – for transport, in particular. Colani starts from the principle that it's quite simple to design a motorbike: it would be enough to ask "a guy to climb aboard a lump of clay roughly hacked out to the size of the bike, and to settle down onto it comfortably. Then all you have to do is to sculpt the bodywork taking account of the impression he's left behind." He designed the prototype of this Yamaha racing bike in 1986, during a period spent in Japan (1982-1986), when he worked for Canon and Yamaha among others. This machine – which did not in the end go into production – is remarkable for the rounded, curvilinear forms of its integral fairing in red fibreglass that almost entirely covers the rider, who must more or less lie down on the bike, becoming one with the machine – as did rider Urs Wenger when, in Italy on 7 December 1986, he broke the world speed record (reaching an unofficial maximum of 336 km/h) with this prototype • **MTMR**

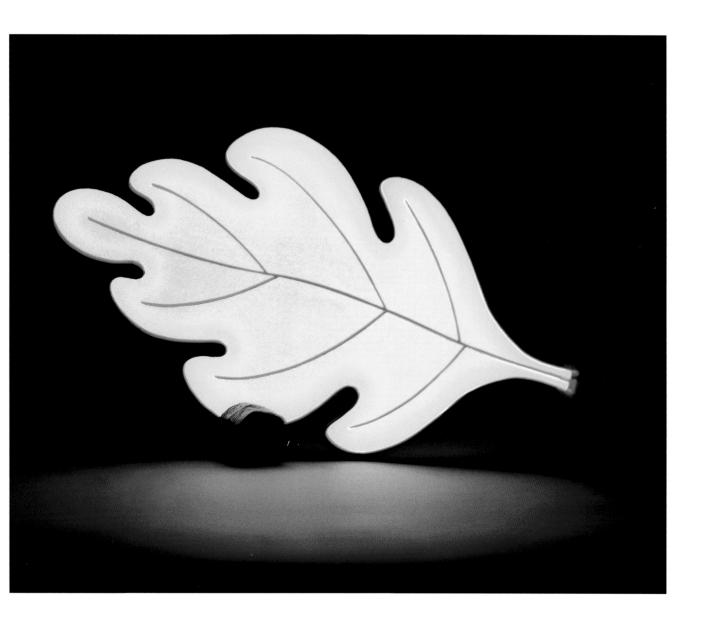

Andrea Branzi

| 1938, Florence (Italy)

• • • • • • • • • • • • • • • • • •

Andrea Branzi was a founding member of Archizoom Associates, of anti-design research and education group Global Tools and of Studio Alchimia. In 1981, he joined the Memphis Group, developing a notion of design based on the quest for the expressive, as opposed to Modernism's "objectivity" and "reduction of the semantic." The design of the *Foglia* electroluminescent lamp demonstrates the importance that Branzi accords to form, to image indeed, even as the lamp denies nothing of its function. Resting on a section of branch, the luminous "leaf" is delicately tinted in shades of yellow and green, while the stylised veins underline the reference. This archetypal, friendly object testifies to the designer's ambition to bring together the two apparently opposed registers of the natural and the technological, here successfully reconciled. The same might be said of his *Domestic Animals* series (1985), in which he combines industrial and natural materials: a floor lamp, for example, consisting of a double cone of aluminium fixed to a roundel of wood, or a bench with a minimalist, geometrical seat but a back of irregular natural birch branch • **PT**

⬆ **1988**

Foglia Lamp
Manufacturer: Memphis (Italy)
Acrylic glass
45 cm x 25 cm x 1 mm
Gift of Strafor (Strasbourg, France), 1999 - AM 1999-1-6

Marc Newson

| 1963, Sydney (Australia)

• • • • • • • • • • • • • • • • •

The Australian Marc Newson grew up on the beachfront, in a country without an indigenous design tradition, a background that gave him the freedom to explore the unusual. His liking for aluminium was evident when he constructed his first piece, by hand, in a garage: the *Lockheed Lounge Chair* (1986), riveted together like an aeroplane fuselage. Its voluptuous lines reflect some of the designer's diverse sources of inspiration: surfing, aeronautics, and organic forms, almost human. Newson is also mad about cars. Like all his other aluminium pieces since he settled in London, he had the *Alufelt* chair made by panel beaters

Bodylines, specialists in the restoration of the Aston Martin cars the designer loves. Formed by hand on a jig, like a wing or a bonnet, the *Alufelt* offers a variety of unaccustomed sensual experiences: the gleam of the aluminium, the hollow body that hides nothing, the hole in the middle that turns into a single back leg. The reverse is painted in one of three different shades: Aston Martin green, Ferrari red or Marc Newson's own favourite orange. A version is available in fibreglass from Italian manufacturers Cappellini, and one in wicker from a Japanese furniture maker. Marc Newson's often sculptural style brings his design close to art, and he is now the best-selling designer in the world's auction houses • **XJ**

⊕ **1993**

Alufelt Chair
Made for Pod (Italy) by
Bodylines (United Kingdom)
Aluminium
85 x 67 x 100 cm
Purchase, 2001 - AM 2001-1-153

Maarten Van Severen

1956, Antwerp (Belgium)
2005, Ghent (Belgium)

• • • • • • • • • • • • • • • • •

The designer Maarten Van Severen refused to be called a "minimalist." He was right, for his *LC95* chair is the fruit of a patient search for the right solution, simultaneously formal and technical. It consists of a single, thin sheet of folded aluminium, its two ends joined by rubber spacers, that seems to hover in the air. Waxed, the chair may gain a patina with time, a distinctive feature of his creations. Maarten Van Severen was a designer who remained stubbornly resistant to the lyrical or extraverted. Son of the painter and sculptor Dan Van Severen, he studied architecture before embarking on a design career in 1980. For seven years, he brought his lucid line to furniture he designed and made with his own tools, for himself and for family and friends. He also worked with Dutch architect Rem Koolhaas, collaborating on the interior of the Lemoine House, near Bordeaux, for which he designed the spectacular lift-cum-study. He then began a collaboration with Swiss furniture manufacturers Vitra. One of his chairs, the humble and discreet *03* was developed there for mass production, and is now to be found both in fast food outlets and in Ghent cathedral. The *LC95* is still in production, available in aluminium from Aiki, or in transparent methacrylate from Kartell. Considered to be the greatest Belgian designer, Maarten Van Severen died of cancer at the age of 48 • **XJ**

⬆ **1993-1995**

Low Chair LC95
Manufacturer: Top Mouton (Belgium)
Aluminium
63 x 92 x 50 cm
Gift of the Société des Amis du Musée National d'Art Moderne (Paris, France), 2001
AM 2001-1-142

James Dyson

| 1947, Cromer (United Kingdom)

• • • • • • • • • • • • • • • • • • • •

The Dyson vacuum cleaner is one of the most remarkable successes in industrial design – the idea of one man winning out against the opinion of marketing men and manufacturers. By the early 1980s, British designer James Dyson, a graduate of the Royal College of Art, already had a number of inventions to his credit, such as the all-terrain wheelbarrow with a spherical wheel. It was in thinking about a new air filter system installed at the factory making this barrow that he had the idea of applying the same principle to a vacuum cleaner, the dust no longer being sucked into a bag but separated from the air by centrifugal force. In 1986, after 5,127 prototypes, a first

enormously expensive model was marketed in Japan under the G-Force brand. The first Dyson, an upright cleaner called the *DC01*, came out in 1993, to be followed by a cylinder version, the *DC02*. In looks too, they were the opposite of everything that was done at the time: rather than hiding the mechanism under a more-or-less "aesthetic" housing, Dyson left it visible in all its glory, done out in bright colours, the dust-collection bin itself being of transparent plastic. Despite high prices, the Dyson brand became the leader on the English market, and a great international success. In 2009, James Dyson revolutionised another device when he introduced the bladeless fan. These two inventions demonstrate how design can be a means to effective innovation • **XJ**

⬙ **1997**

DC02 Clear Vacuum Cleaner

Manufacturer: Dyson (United Kingdom)
ABS and polycarbonate
41 x 30 x 52 cm
Gift of Dyson (Malmesbury, United Kingdom), 2001 - AM 2000-1-87

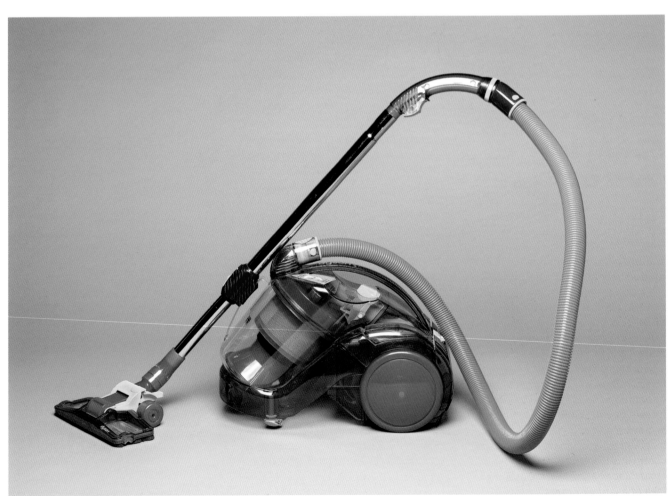

Philippe Starck

| 1949, Paris (France)

The first transparent chair moulded in a single piece resulted from the collaboration between Philippe Starck and Italian manufacturer Kartell. The production of *La Marie* coincided with a revival in the use of plastic for furniture, following a fall in the price of oil. Tough and flexible, polycarbonate replaced the Plexiglas used in the 1960s, more liable to crack or scratch. The designer had already been an international star for a decade, and he was embarking on a phase in which he said he no longer wanted to produce signature pieces, but archetypes. With its go-anywhere design, the *La Marie* chair thus looks like people's idea of a chair, just as *Miss Sissi* is everyone's idea of a lamp. At the same time, with

La Redoute, Starck launched his *Good Goods* range of "honest and responsible" products sold by mail order: in it, *La Marie* was joined by a biodynamic champagne, a vegetable-based detergent... Starck prophesied a dematerialisation of the object, of which this chair was intended as a foretaste. The catalogue came out in 1999, and though they had but little influence at the time, many of its ideas on the moralization of the market economy are still relevant today. Also for Kartell, the designer would pursue his interest in transparency with the *Louis Ghost* (2002) and *Victoria Ghost* (2005) chairs, which achieved enormous commercial success • **XJ**

⚐ 1998

La Marie Chair
Manufacturer: Kartell (Italy)
Polycarbonate
88 x 50 x 52 cm
Gift of Kartell (Noviglio, Italy),
1999 - AM 1999-1-161

Ronan & Erwan Bouroullec

Ronan Bouroullec

| 1971, Quimper (France)

Erwan Bouroullec

| 1976, Quimper (France)

• • • • • • • • • • • • • • •

The Bouroullec brothers have always come up with pieces halfway between furniture and architecture. This one provides a bedroom without need for walls. Conceived as a self-assembly kit, it has something of the little houses that children improvise for themselves, a suggestion of caravan… Some have seen in it a reinterpretation of the traditional box-bed of the brothers' native Brittany, but they say they weren't thinking of that when they made it. Production of this prototype was supported by an award from VIA (Valorisation de l'Innovation dans l'Ameublement). When it was shown, its media impact was enormous, and pictures of the UFO-bed were everywhere in the magazines. Even if only twelve were ever manufactured, it has become a playful symbol of mobility and flexibility at time when apartments, like offices, are tending to become open-plan. It made a name for its designers, who continue today to combine experiment with industrial production. The Bouroullecs have also created other miniature architectural spaces: a little house of polystyrene, an indoor hut, a floating house… Their researches have led to mass-produced furniture intended to improve life in the open-plan office, the alcove-sofa of 2007, for example, and their serious yet poetical approach has won for the two brothers a world-wide reputation • **XJ**

⬆ **2000**

Lit clos

Prototype
Manufactured for Galerie kreo (France) by Ufacto (France)
Steel, wood, resin and metal

Bed
214 x 240 x 140 cm

Legs
70 cm (h)

Donated by VIA/Valorisation de l'Innovation dans l'Ameublement (Paris, France), 2009 - AM 2010-1-73

Tokujin Yoshioka

| 1967, Saga (Japan)

• • • • • • • • • • • • • • •

⤵ **2001**

Honey-pop Chairs
Manufacturer: Tokujin Yoshioka
Design (Japan)
Concertina-folded paper
83 x 80 x 74 cm (unfolded)
62 x 75 x 2 cm (folded)
0.4 kg (weight)
Gift of the artist, 2003
AM 2002-1-27

Born on the island of Kyūshū, Tokujin Yoshioka studied at the Kuwasawa Design School in Tokyo. He worked for a year for Shirō Kuramata, who recommended him to Issey Miyake: between 1988 and 2000, he designed Miyake's window displays, shops, showrooms and exhibitions, including the much remarked-on "Making Things" at the Fondation Cartier in Paris, in 1998-1999. In 2000, he established his own office, Tokujin Yoshioka Design, going on to design further window displays for A-Poc, Hermès, Shiseido, Muji, Toyota, Nissan, BMW and Peugeot. The *Honey-pop* chair with its honeycomb paper structure brought him his first success in 2001. The following year it was shown by Driade at the Milan Furniture Fair, together with his "Tokyo-pop" series (sofa, armchair, lounge chair, small table, high table and stool) in rotomoulded polyethylene. Its process of production is both innovative and poetical. Prioritizing economy of means and gesture, Yoshioka cuts a single form from a one-centimetre-thick rectangle of concertina-folded glassine paper, consisting of 120 layers. The user then expands this as if it were a Chinese lantern, and the form is crushed into closer conformity to the body as one sits on it. The user's own weight and tactile experience thus form an integral part of the process of the chair's creation. It is in human sensual experience and in features of nature – void, lightness, shadow and impermanence – that Yoshioka finds inspiration for his always-astonishing creations • **OR**

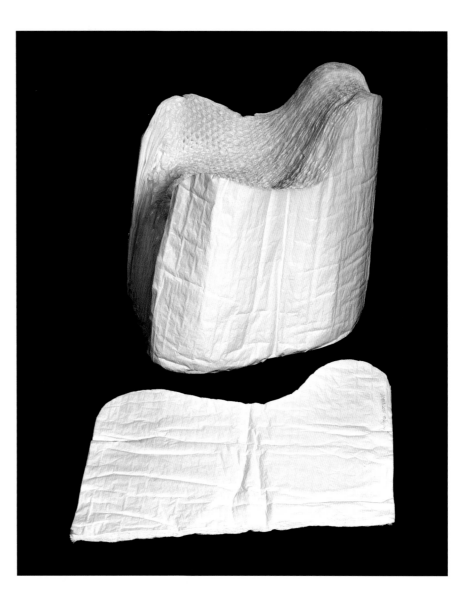

⬆ **2004**

Solid C2 Chair
Manufacturer: Materialise
(Belgium)
Epoxy resin
77 x 40 x 54 cm
Gift of MGX by Materialise
(Louvain, Belgium), 2010
AM 2010-1-9

Patrick Jouin

| 1967, Nantes (France)

• • • • • • • • • • • • • • • • • • • •

Refusing to recognize boundaries, Patrick Jouin has exploded the conventions in every field of design, from high-tech to high-quality artisan production. In 2004, he began to use rapid prototyping techniques, until then thought of as no more than means of validating a design, for manufacturing the finished product. Using computer-aided design (CAD) software, he could thus produce three-dimensional objects without any mould-making.

Part of the "Solid" furniture collection, the *C2* chair was produced for Agence Patrick Jouin by the Belgian company Materialise, using an SLA (Selective Laser Activation) stereolithography technique, whereby a photosensitive plastic – a liquid epoxy resin – is hardened by the effect of a laser. Guided by the CAD file, the chair – designed as a single piece requiring no assembly at all – is built up in a vat of resin, which is polymerized by the laser beam and so solidified at the locations required. The operation takes nine days. Jouin has said that he was inspired, in designing the chair, by long stems of grass leaning in all directions and all mixed up together. This is a chair that escapes classification • **MD**

Junya Ishigami

1974, Kanagawa (Japan)

. . . .

After graduating in architecture and town planning at the University of Fine Arts in Tokyo, Junya Ishigami worked for four years at Sejima and Nishizawa and Associates (SANAA), where he honed his skills on architectural projects of the greatest economy, simplicity and sophistication. In 2004, he set up his own firm, Junya Ishigami Architect & Associates, in Tokyo. That same year he designed the *Low Chair*, with matching circular coffee table. It is laser-cut from a single block of white polystyrene foam. Like a skin, a subtle guipure lace covers the surface of the chair, giving the piece an artisanal aspect that complements its high technology. The name of the chair is a reference to the fine engineering of the Lexus marque, established by the Toyota Motor Corporation in 1987. The chair combines the quest for lightness with monochromatically minimal effects. The expression of a brand image, the chair was shown at the Milan Furniture Fair in 2005. The much-noticed presentation played on light and shadow, emphasizing fragility, phenomenality and evanescence. Wonderfully combining technological forms and strange, dream-like worlds, Ishigami has won a world-wide reputation for exhibition designs and architectural spaces, all purity and transparency ● **OR**

⬇ 2005

Low Chair
Produced by MINERVA Inc.
Manufactured by MITUISI
Polystyrene and cotton guipure lace
45 x 52 x 57 cm
Gift of the Toyota Motor
Corporation (Aichi, Japan), 2007
AM 2007-1-2

Demakersvan

Jeroen Verhoeven
| 1976, Tegelen (Netherlands)

Joep Verhoeven
| 1976, Tegelen (Netherlands)

Judith de Graauw
| 1976, Schaijk (Netherlands)

Group formed in 2004

· · · · · · · · · · · · · · · · ·

Having graduated together from the Design Academy Eindhoven, in Holland, brothers Jeroen and Joep Verhoeven and Judith de Graauw founded the Demakersvan collective (literally, "the makers of") in 2004. Their studio, where they produce their own early prototypes, is in Rotterdam. Their projects focus on properly mass-produced objects that nonetheless involve craft skills. They thus combine the use of numerically controlled machine tools and the latest technologies with a very precise hand finish. The *Cinderella* table illustrates this hybridization of the two approaches. The designers have here reinterpreted in three dimensions drawings of 17th- and 18th-century French furniture found in the archives of the Rijksmuseum, Amsterdam, the curves of tables and chests of drawers being treated in the manner of a fictive, romanticized past, as is suggested by the name "Cinderella."

Constructed from 57 "slices" of birch ply, cut, carefully assembled and glued by hand, the piece stands on three legs and presents three distinct faces. The first "solid" aspect, half-table and half-chest, evidences a remarkable play on the layers, folds and curves of the plywood, while the two others, "hollow," reveal, like biological sections, the baroque lines and volumes within. The Centre Pompidou's *Cinderella* table is the ninth of a series limited to twenty. Six further examples were later produced in Carrara marble • **OR**

⬇ 2005

Cinderella Table
Birch plywood
80 x 132 x 101 cm
Purchase, supported by Mrs Tomoko Yamaguchi, 2008
AM 2008-1-102

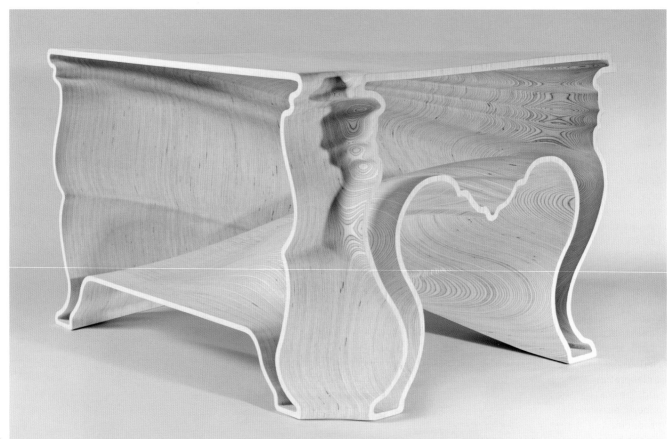

Ron Arad

| 1951, Tel Aviv (Israel)

• • • • • • • • • • • • • • • • • •

Fascinated by new techniques, Ron Arad is tireless in his exploration of the most sophisticated technologies, experimenting with materials as various as steel, carbon fibre, Corian® and silicone. In 2002, he designed *Oh-Void 1* for the "Paperwork" series, a rocking chaise longue composed of two sinusoidal ellipses. This first version was constructed in a composite material with an aramid fibre honeycomb core, whose toughness and lightness made it possible to shift the chair's centre of gravity. In 2004, in collaboration with Du Pont de Nemours and The Gallery Mourmans, he experimented with new techniques, producing the chairs by using acrylate glue to bond together moulded and polished sheets of Corian®, a material whose translucency helps retain an effect of lightness even though the piece weighs around 180 kg. The *Oh-Void 2* can be coloured – red for example – or lines of colour and transparency can alternate.

Designed in 2006, the Centre's chair was the model of a series of six, part of the "Blo-Glo" collection. Through the moulded silicone, one sees the internal structure of steel, a curious spine that emphasizes by contrast the mass of this sculptural volume. On this skeleton, Ron Arad has inscribed his motto: "There is no solution because there is no problem." In 2006 and 2008 there followed coloured versions in cut and polished acrylic. Most of these pieces have been made available in limited editions by The Gallery Mourmans • **MD**

⚐ **2006**

Oh-Void Chair
"Blo-Glo" series
Silicone and metal
70 x 120 x 65 cm
Purchase, 2006 - AM 2006-1-62

Louise Campbell

| 1970, Copenhagen (Denmark)

• • • • • • • • • • • • • • • • • •

The child of Danish and English parents, Louise Campbell graduated from the London College of Furniture in 1992 before returning to Denmark to gain a diploma in industrial design in 1995. A year later, she set up her own studio, designing interiors, lighting and high-tech furniture for clients such as Louis Poulsen, Zanotta, HAY, Royal Copenhagen and Muuto. Her furniture is known for its generous and airy forms, playful, elegant and very graphic. She designed the *Veryround Chair* for the Italian firm Zanotta in 2006. Produced from two-millimetre-thick sheet steel using a 3D laser cutter, the two-layer structure presents a pattern of intersecting circles that increase in size from the centre to the circumference. The largest circles at the edge are bent over, holding the two layers apart. Only the tube that joins them at the centre is of a different, trellis-like pattern. The repetition of the circle motif and the effects of light and shadow produced on the ground give this chair a highly sophisticated, elegant yet playful lightness. The white colour, too, emphasizes its diaphanous character. The chair exists in nine numbered and signed examples, painted in different colours • **OR**

⊘ 2006

Veryround Chair
Manufacturer: Zanotta (Italy)
Steel
70 x 110 x 88 cm
Gift of Zanotta (Nova Milanese, Italy), 2009 - AM 2009-1-30

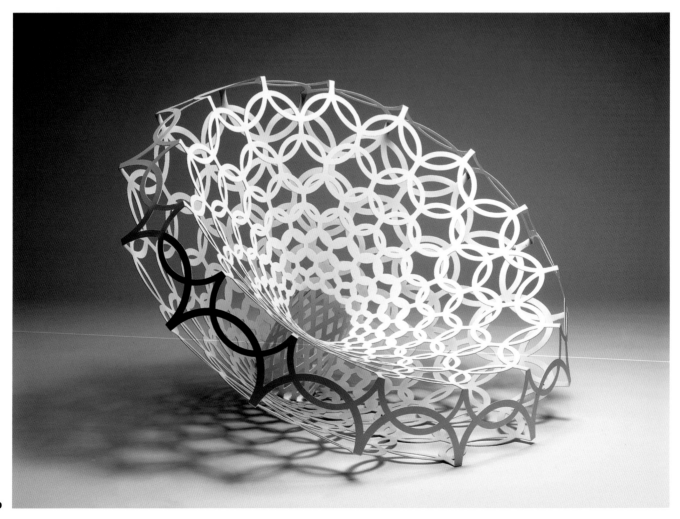

2006

G Mirror
"Platform" collection
Manufacturer: Galerie kreo
(France)
Stainless steel
127 x 90 cm
Gift of the Société des Amis du
Musée National d'Art Moderne
(Paris, France), 2011 - EC2011-1-DE4

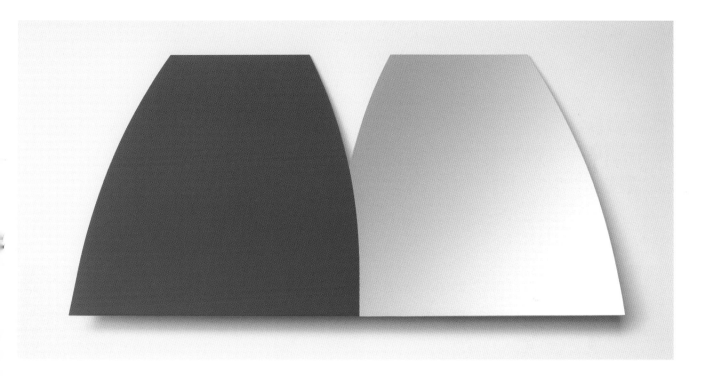

Pierre Charpin

1962, Saint-Mandé (France)

• • • • • • • • • • • • • • • • • • •

This mirror was made for the "Platform" exhibition at Galerie kreo in 2006, where it complemented a series of low tables in aluminium. Pseudo-Minimalist, it consists of two almost identical forms in stainless steel sheet, one polished to perfection, the other painted, the two surfaces offering different qualities of reflection. "One's experience of one's own reflected image is diversified," explains the designer. If in a bad mood, one can stand in front of the coloured side, where only a silhouette will be visible… The G mirror is typical of Pierre Charpin's work, with which one is never sure what one is looking at. Trained at the École des Beaux-Arts in Bourges, he approaches design with the distinctive sensibility of the visual artist. He does not however forget the functional aspect: a table remains a table, a vase a vase, yet they always reflect the personality of the designer in subtle little details, a very personal sense of colour and an emphasis on the sensuality of materials. For Pierre Charpin, design is above all the outcome of an encounter: nothing is totally fixed in advance, and a piece develops gradually in dialogue with a retailer or manufacturer. While the designer is more interested in "series of objects" than "objects in series," he also enjoys designing mass-market products, such as the *Eau de Paris* water jug, 90,000 of which have been produced since 2005 • **XJ**

Joris Laarman

| 1979, Borculo (Netherlands)

• • • • • • • • • • • • • • • • • • •

Having graduated form the Design Academy Eindhoven in 2003, Joris Laarman established his own studio in Rotterdam, where he designs and makes most of his pieces. He works with important furniture manufacturers – Droog, Jaga, Flos, Vitra – and also leads seminars at major European schools of architecture and design.

It was for a special joint presentation by the Droog Design Foundation and the Barry Friedman gallery at Design Miami in 2006 that Laarman created the first two pieces of the "Bone Furniture" series, a chair and a chaise longue. There he drew inspiration from the growth of bone structure, and from the biological sciences more generally, to develop a new range of diverse forms. Using a high-tech digital tool developed by car manufacturer Adam Opel GmbH, he could create elegant and complex sculptural objects as single wholes. The series explores the technical and aesthetic properties of different materials, from aluminium, or the marble of the first chairs, to the UV-resistant polyurethane resin used in this prototype.

Placing his use of new technologies in a cultural context, Joris Laarman also makes reference here to Charles and Ray Eames *La Chaise* of 1948, an icon of biomorphic design. This *Lounge Chair* was made in a limited edition of twelve • OR

⬇ 2006

Lounge Chair
"Bone Furniture" series
Prototype
Polyurethane resin
77.3 x 100 x 158 cm
Purchase, 2008 - AM 2008-1-66

Black Mirror One
Manufacturer: Galerie kreo
(France)
Silicon carbide
50 x 26 x 1.5 cm
Gift of M. Olivier Diaz (Paris,
France), 2011 - EC2011-1-DE-3

Martin Szekely

| 1956, Paris (France)

· · · · · · · · · · · · · · · · · · · ·

This mirror absorbs colour, only 60% of
incident light being reflected. It recalls
the Claude mirror, named for the
painter Claude Lorrain (1602-1682): made
of tinted glass, this would bring out the
major lines and volumes in a scene.
This project is part of Martin Szekely's
"investigation of limits." Here, the limit
is the highest quality of reflected image
currently available, the real world
looking less clear and distinct than its
reflection in the *Black Mirror One*. To
achieve this, it was necessary to polish
a silicon carbide surface for a month.
Structurally similar to diamond, this
material exists as stardust, and it is
produced artificially to make the
mirrors sent into space by NASA in
order to observe the cosmos. Boostec
Industries of Tarbes, France, is a
specialist in their manufacture, and
they made Szekely's mirror. Exploring
the limits of the possible – in a
philosophical rather than a technical
sense – is today the designer's chief
concern, and it is in this spirit that he
has also produced tables in the light
concrete called Ductal • **XJ**

List of works

Otto Wagner
Chair, 1900-1906.................................p. 14

Peter Behrens
Electric Kettle, 1909-1910 ....p. 14

Atelier Gras
Office Lamp, No 211, 1922...................p. 16

Pierre Chareau
Floor Lamp, known as the
" Grande Religieuse, " 1923 ....p. 17

Joost Schmidt
"Staatliches Bauhaus" Poster, 1923 ....p. 18

Josef Hartwig
Chess Set, 1923-1924.............................p. 19

Marcel Breuer
Dining Room Suite for Wassily Kandinsky,
1926..p. 20

Jacques Le Chevallier
Sphère No 4/6 Lamp, [1927] ....p. 21

Robert Mallet-Stevens
Chair, [1927] ....p. 22

Pierre Chareau
Desk for Robert Mallet-Stevens,
1927 ....p. 23

Henri Liber
M42 Rebil Chair, 1927 ....p. 25

Charlotte Perriand
Extending Table, 1927 ....p. 25

Francis Jourdain
Rail-Mounted Furniture, 1927-1928 ....p. 26

Eileen Gray
Bathroom Cupboard, 1927-1929 ....p. 27

Eileen Gray
Transat Chair, 1927-1929 ....p. 28

**Le Corbusier, Charlotte Perriand,
Pierre Jeanneret**
Grand Confort Chair, 1928............................p. 29

Giuseppe Pagano
Tub Chair, 1928.....................................p. 31

Djo-Bourgeois
Desk, 1929..p. 31

René Herbst
Desk, 1929...p. 32

Louis Sognot
Bar Stool, 1929 ....p. 33

Jean Prouvé
Reclining Chair, [1929-1930]...........................p. 34

Émile Guillot
B 257 Chair, 1930................................p. 35

André Lurçat
B 327 Desk, 1930 ....p. 36

Jean Prouvé
Grand Repos Chair, 1930...............................p. 37

Alvar Aalto
Paimio Chair, 1930-1931.......................p. 38

René Herbst
Chair, 1931..p. 39

Robert Mallet-Stevens
Chair, 1931...p. 40

Gerrit Rietveld
Zigzag Chair, 1932-1933 ....p. 40

Marcel Breuer
Chaise longue, 1932-1934...................p. 42

Eugène Beaudouin, Marcel Lods
Chaise longue pour le repos, 1934-1935 .... p. 43

Gio Ponti
Chair, 1936-1938..................................p. 44

René Coulon
Radiaver Electric Heater, 1937 ....p. 45

Hans Coray
Landi Chair, 1938................................p. 46

Charlotte Perriand
Table en forme, 1938 ....p. 47

Bruno Mathsson
Pernilla Chaise Longue, 1943......................p. 48

Eero Saarinen
Womb Chair, 1946-1947........................p. 49

Charles Eames, Ray Eames
Paw Chair, 1948 ....p. 50

Bic
Bic Cristal, 1950...................................p. 51

Carlo Mollino
Desk, 1950...p. 52

Hans J. Wegner
Dolphin Chaise Longue, 1950.....................p. 53

Marco Zanuso
Lady Chair, 1951.................................p. 54

Harry Bertoia
Diamond Chair, 1952.........................p. 55

Janette Laverrière
Wall-Mounted Bureau, 1952 ....p. 56

Poul Kjærholm
Fireside Chair, 1953-1954..................p. 57

Serge Mouille
Wall Light, 1953-1958.........................p. 58

Willy Guhl
Garden Chair, 1954.............................p. 59

Gino Sarfatti
Floor Lamp (model 1063), 1954.......p. 60

Isamu Noguchi
Lamps 10A and 3A, [1955] ....p. 61

Osvaldo Borsani
P40 Armchair, 1955 ....p. 62

Poul Henningsen
Wall Lamp, 1955..................................p. 63

Le Corbusier
Atelier Le Corbusier Kitchen Type 1, 1955..p. 64

Janine Abraham, Dirk Jan Rol
Fireside Chair, 1956 ....p. 65

George Nelson
DAF Chair, 1956 ....p. 66

Arne Jacobsen
Drop Chair, 1958..................................p. 66

Pierre Guariche
Vallée Blanche Chaise Longue, 1960.........p. 68

**Achille Castiglioni,
Pier Giacomo Castiglioni**
Toio Floor Lamp, 1962 ....p. 69

Dieter Rams
T1000 Radio, 1962...............................p. 70

Joe Colombo
La Sella Chair, 1963.............................p. 71

Roger Tallon
Portavia P 111 Television, 1963 ....p. 72

Olivier Mourgue
Two-Seater Sofa, 1964-1965 ....p. 73

Richard Sapper, Marco Zanuso
Grillo Telephone, 1965........................p. 74

Pierre Paulin
Ribbon Chair (model 582), 1966 ....p. 75

Gae Aulenti
Ruspa Lamp, 1967................................p. 76

Haus-Rucker-Co
Mindexpander 1, 1967.........................p. 77

Marc Held
Culbuto Chair, 1967 ....p. 78

Ugo La Pietra
Globo Tissurato Lamp, 1967...............p. 78

Archizoom Associati
Safari Sofa, 1968..................................p. 80

Pierre Paulin
Déclive, 1968..p. 81

Ettore Sottsass
Altare (Molto Privato), 1968..............p. 82

Superstudio
Gherpe Lamp, 1968...............................p. 83

Ettore Sottsass
Pilastro Totem, 1969 ....p. 84

Mario Bellini
Teneride Chair, 1970 ....p. 85

Shiro Kuramata
Side 1 and Side 2, 1970.......................p. 86

Verner Panton
Living Sculpture, 1970-1971 ....p. 87

Jean Widmer
"Design français" Poster, 1971.......p. 88

Oscar Niemeyer
Chair, 1972...p. 89

Gaetano Pesce
Golgotha Chair, 1972...........................p. 90

Michel Cadestin
Traîneau Chair, 1976 ....p. 91

Alessandro Mendini
Kandissi Sofa, 1979.............................p. 92

Roman Cieslewicz
"Paris-Paris 1937-1957" Poster, 1981............p. 93

Garouste & Bonetti
Barbare Chair, 1981.............................p. 94

Martin Szekely
Pi Chaise Longue, 1982-1983 ....p. 95

Michele De Lucchi
Tolomeo Table Lamp, 1983 .... p. 96

Philippe Starck
J. Armchair, 1984 .... p. 97

Luigi Colani
Racing Motorcycle, 1986 .... p. 98

Andrea Branzi
Foglia Lamp, 1988 .... p. 99

Marc Newson
Alufelt Chair, 1993 .... p. 100

Maarten Van Severen
Low Chair LC95, 1993-1995 .... p. 101

James Dyson
DC02 Clear Vacuum Cleaner, 1997 .... p. 102

Philippe Starck
La Marie Chair, 1998 .... p. 103

Ronan & Erwan Bouroullec
Lit clos, 2000 .... p. 104

Tokujin Yoshioka
Honey-pop Chairs, 2001 .... p. 105

Patrick Jouin
Solid C2 Chair, 2004 .... p. 106

Junya Ishigami
Low Chair, 2005 .... p. 107

Demakersvan
Cinderella Table, 2005 .... p. 108

Ron Arad
Oh-Void Chair, 2006 .... p. 109

Louise Campbell
Veryround Chair, 2006 .... p. 110

Pierre Charpin
G Mirror, 2006 .... p. 111

Joris Laarman
Lounge Chair, 2006 .... p. 112

Martin Szekely
Black Mirror One, 2007 .... p. 113

Photographic credits
© Centre Pompidou,
MNAM-CCI/ photos :
Jacques Faujour ;
Georges Meguerditchian ;
Philippe Migeat ;
Jean-Claude Planchet ;
Bertrand Prévost
/Dist.RMN-GP

First printed in
September 2011
by the Artegrafica,
Graphicom Group in
Verona
Printed in Italy